"This book sho... reveals how the ... ing of our own ... own resiliency will help us thrive in our ever-changing and growingly complicated world. This book will help you settle down *and* settle in to the deeper and more tenacious part of who you are—the part you have probably been looking for all along."

> —**Tim Ryan,** US representative, Ohio, and
> author of *A Mindful Nation*

"Inviting, wise, and practical. A must-read for those new to mindfulness and longtime MBSR graduates, alike. *MBSR Every Day* will inspire you to be your best self, to live fully, and to stay motivated to 'just do it' and practice mindfulness every day."

> —**Susan Bauer-Wu, PhD, RN**, Tussi and
> John Kluge Endowed Professor in
> contemplative end-of-life care at the
> University of Virginia School of Nursing,
> and author of *Leaves Falling Gently*

"If you are looking for a practical and easy-to-read guide to applying the wisdom of the mindfulness-based stress reduction (MBSR) program to your everyday life, this book is for you. Elisha Goldstein and Bob Stahl have teamed up to offer an invaluable treasure trove of scientifically proven techniques we can apply to the everyday hassles and challenges of our busy modern lives. I highly recommend this book for novice practitioners, as well as experienced meditators who want to revitalize their practices."

—**Patricia A. Jennings, MEd, PhD**, associate professor at the Curry School of Education, University of Virginia, and author of *Mindfulness for Teachers*

"With clarity and simplicity, the authors outline practical strategies for living an inspired, connected, and openhearted life—one with balance, steadiness, and wisdom amidst the inevitable joys and sorrows. Highly recommended."

—**Tara Healey, MEd**, program director of Mindfulness-Based Learning at Harvard Pilgrim Health Care

"Elisha Goldstein and Bob Stahl convey the sweetness and depth that can be found by bringing awareness to the simple activities and experiences of a typical modern life. Beginners and longtime practitioners alike will be inspired by the doorways that lead to deep inner truths."

> —**Megan Cowan**, cofounder of
> Mindful Schools

"This is a book worth carrying around with you. It's a rich treasury of easily digestible practices that can help make mindfulness an everyday refreshing habit rather than a dutiful chore. It's also filled with helpful background research and insightful commentary."

> —**Barry Boyce**, editor-in-chief of *Mindful*
> (mindful.org)

"Take one amazing program that has brought relief to thousands of people across the planet, add two wise and warm teachers with deep experience and clarity of expression, blend them together with compassion and practicality, and you have this book: a shining gem that distills the essence of MBSR into simple yet powerful reflections, exercises, and practices. Just as MBSR is a collection of moments, so is this book. Clear, helpful, kindhearted, and practical, *MBSR Every Day* is a valuable guide to anyone who seeks to live a more mindful life."

—**Steven D. Hickman, PsyD**, clinical psychologist, executive director at the UCSD Center for Mindfulness, and associate clinical professor in the UCSD department of psychiatry

"Authors Goldstein and Stahl teach us how to cultivate a mindful, heartful awareness with great simplicity and mastery. Giving yourself to the practices offered in this clear, wise, easy-to-use book is truly a gift to the soul. Enjoy!"

—**Tara Brach, PhD**, author of *Radical Acceptance* and *True Refuge*

MBSR Every Day

Daily Practices from the Heart of Mindfulness-Based Stress Reduction

♦ ♦ ♦

ELISHA GOLDSTEIN, PhD
BOB STAHL, PhD

New Harbinger Publications, Inc.

Publisher's Note

This publication is designed to provide accurate and authoritative information in regard to the subject matter covered. It is sold with the understanding that the publisher is not engaged in rendering psychological, financial, legal, or other professional services. If expert assistance or counseling is needed, the services of a competent professional should be sought.

Distributed in Canada by Raincoast Books

Copyright © 2015 by Elisha Goldstein and Bob Stahl
New Harbinger Publications, Inc.
5674 Shattuck Avenue
Oakland, CA 94609
www.newharbinger.com

Cover design by Amy Shoup; Interior design by Michele Waters-Kermes; Acquired by Jess O'Brien; Edited by Jennifer Eastman

Library of Congress Cataloging-in-Publication Data on file

MIX
Paper from
responsible sources
FSC
www.fsc.org
FSC® C011935

Printed in the United States of America

17   16   15

10 9 8 7 6 5 4 3 2 1   First printing

This book is dedicated to all who choose to
bring mindfulness into their everyday lives.
This makes the world a better place to live in.

Contents

Part 2: Breathe

Part 3: Tune the Heart

Part 4: Meditate

Part 5: Be

Introduction

This is a book of essential practices that lie at the heart of the most widely embraced mindfulness-based programs available in the world today, mindfulness-based stress reduction (MBSR). Within these pages, you'll find simple ways to bring the science, art, and practice of MBSR into your daily life to decrease suffering and bring you greater balance and peace. You'll learn some new practices for how to *find patience, find gifts in imperfection, make peace with your mind and body, trust your experience, cultivate self-compassion, love yourself, meditate, break free from negative thoughts,* and *feel more connected.*

We want to affirm that you are an active participant in your health and well-being and that allowing this book to be your companion in the days ahead is a great act of self-care—some may even say self-love. Why? It's no longer news that how we pay attention and what we pay attention to not only affects our lives but also shapes our brains. When it comes to MBSR, the findings consistently point to the fact that these practices change your mind, body, and life for the better. They:

- increase immune functioning under stress (Davidson et al. 2003)

- improve resiliency with the brain's ability to process emotions under stress (Davidson et al. 2003)

- increase gray matter in the insula and cortex of the brain (Hölzel et al. 2011)

- reduce chronic pain (Kabat-Zinn et al. 1998; Rosenzweig et al. 2010)

- improve *eudaimonia*, or psychological well-being (Fredrickson et al. 2013)

- naturally increase empathy, self-compassion, and compassion (Shapiro, Schwartz, and Bonner 1998; Shapiro et al. 2005)

- decrease anxiety (Miller, Fletcher, and Kabat-Zinn 1995) and obsessive compulsive disorder (Baxter et al. 1992)

- prevent relapse into depression (Teasdale et al. 2000; Segal et al. 2010)

- prevent relapse with drug addiction (Parks, Anderson, and Marlatt 2001)

- enhance quality of life even under stress-related chronic illness (Carlson et al. 2007).

There is a saying in MBSR: no matter what you're dealing with, as long as you are living and breathing, there is far more right with you than wrong with you. But much of the time, it seems that our minds tell us a different story. This internal narrative is often about what's wrong with us, how we compare to others around us, or why we're deficient or defective in some way—or, sometimes, maybe why we're so amazing. These stories are often at the heart of what drives the suffering we experience in daily life. One of the greatest gifts of mindfulness is that we learn from the inside out that we are not our stories, not even the ones that tell us we are. We start to get better and better at recognizing that we have a choice in how we pay attention and what we pay attention to. You have a choice to become awake and *dip beneath the stories, break your routine, let be,* and *practice "kindfulness"*—four of the practices in this book—and then, instead of being stuck in old patterns, you will step into a life of greater freedom and possibility.

So how do you *do it*?

Just Do It!

Even with all the wonderful science and personal accounts of how MBSR has changed people's lives, the reality is that it's completely useless unless we *just do it*.

We can read daily blogs, listen to recordings, or read books continually, but until we actually implement the practices in our lives, it's all fairly useless. Not much changes unless we put the techniques into practice.

When we *just do it*, a whole lot of learning takes place. We experience how a simple practice like coming to your senses can calm a busy mind and bring us back into balance (chapter 2). With practice, we notice a rise in self-compassion (chapter 8), which research has shown is a major factor in preventing a relapse of depression (Neff and Germer 2013). When we bring MBSR as a companion into our lives, we simply begin to feel happier (Carmody and Baer 2008).

But while there are so many compelling reasons to practice, our past conditioning and all the cues from our outside world make it a challenge. We have to have a convincing reason to rise to this challenge. No one is going to do it for us; we have to do this for ourselves.

One way of uncovering your own reason to practice MBSR is by considering what has been going on in your life that led you to pick up *MBSR Every Day*. Are you living with pain or illness? Do you want to learn a way to live better with it? Are you experiencing a high level of stress? Is it a challenge to balance work and personal life? What are you hoping will change as you mindfully engage with the challenges at hand? Maybe you want to gain some clarity, ease stress or pain, gain balance, or create more peace in your life? These intrinsic reasons are the most powerful motivators (Niemiec, Ryan, and Deci 2009); use them to propel yourself to stick to it.

May you see that making time to bring this guidance into your life is an incredible gift to yourself.

Every time you create space to bring this work into your life, you are caring for yourself. As the popular paraphrase of psychologist Donald Hebb's work would have it, "Neurons that fire together wire together." Every time you follow these practices and intentionally take action toward caring about yourself, you build an internal sense that you matter. This is important for all of us, but even more so for those of us who had a childhood of insecurity bred from receiving the opposite message. What would the days, weeks, and months ahead be like if you had a strong sense that you mattered?

Gauge Your Stress

Too many books give you a lot of information about fighting stress but don't give you a way to gauge how effective their advice is in your life. We want you to know how well the practices in this book are working for you, so before moving on to the practices, create an informal assessment about your current stressors. As you integrate the material in this book into your life, you can come back to this assessment and see if you're making progress with your stress.

In a notebook, create a table with four columns. In the first column, list the top five situations that you perceive to be current stressors in your life. They may involve work, school, your spouse, traffic, crowds, being alone, the news, finances, physical pain, unhealthy eating, poor sleep, and so on. The more specific you are, the easier it will be to track your progress. For example, instead of "traffic," you might write, "driving to work in morning traffic," or instead of "my relationship," you might write, "discussing money with my partner."

The other three columns are for your assessment of how much stress these situations cause you (a) now, at the start of your work in this book, (b) midway through the book, and (c) at the end of the book. So in the second column, rate each situation now on a scale of 1 (least stressful) to 10 (most stressful). When you get midway through the book, rate each situation again, and then do it again at the end of the book. This will give you an objective measure to see how this book is supporting you.

For example, John felt a lot of stress on Sunday nights before the workweek began. He noticed his stress rising after dinner, and by the time he was about to go to sleep, his mind was racing through his mental to-do list. When he started the book, he rated this situation as an 8, indicating high stress. As he began to bring awareness to more of the moments in his life, paid attention to his breath, and began to tune into his heart, he reevaluated and found that he was able to calm his busy mind more often, so he rated it as a 5. Toward the end of the book, while his mind would still get active toward bedtime from time to time, he felt much more confident in finding a sense of ease and peace in this situation and rated it a 2. (Note: If you go through your list and find that you're rating all your situations as an 8 or above, it may be wise to use this companion in conjunction with seeing a health care professional.)

In making this assessment, you may find that it's these very stressors that led you to this mindfulness companion. The thirteenth-century Sufi poet Rumi once wrote, "Don't turn your head. / Keep looking at the bandaged place. / That's where the light enters you." Know that the pages that follow will be a guide to using these stressful events to transform the difficulties in your life into your greatest strengths.

How to Use This Book

The writings and practices in this book are based on decades of personal experience and on an exponentially rising number of scientific studies. This can be a lot to sift through for anyone. In this book, we've picked the best of the spirit and practice of MBSR, elements that we know to not only effectively reduce stress and build resilience but also awaken users into a life worth living.

There are several ways to engage this book. You can move through it sequentially, walking alongside this companion in the order we laid out for you. Or, depending on your level or experience of mindfulness practice or the place you are in, you may feel called toward a particular section, like "Tune the Heart" (part 3), and you can begin there. Generally, we recommend taking a few days to a week for each practice, allowing this book to be a yearlong gift of discovery, healing ease, peace, and joy in your life.

In creating this book, we intentionally wrote each chapter in a way that is digestible and doable in daily life. Whatever way you choose to navigate with this companion, *just do it!* You may notice moments of change instantly, or you may feel some impatience, wanting quicker, more dramatic changes. Rest assured that change will come; the key to change is to treat everything with a learning mindset instead of a performance mindset (Dweck 2000, 2006). With a performance mindset, we set ourselves up for getting stuck, because every time we don't meet an expectation, it feels like confirmation that our abilities are fixed. With a learning mindset, even the inevitable setbacks and obstacles are things to be curious about, build upon, and grow from. Both mindsets can lead to change, but only one leads to mastery.

We highly recommend connecting with friends, family members, colleagues, and even strangers in doing this work. People are the best reminders we have to engage in practice. If you don't know anyone who would be interested in doing this work with you, you can go to http://www.mbsrworkbook.com and find a community there. Or go to http://www.meetup.com and see if there is a practice group using this material in your local area. If there isn't a local group already, consider starting one—there may be many others looking to begin a mindfulness practice. In reaching out to others, you not only support yourself but also create ripple effects that heal those around you (and perhaps even the planet).

Begin Again and Again

To modify an old saying, the writings and practices within this book may seem simple, but they're not always easy. Even with the best intentions, you will find yourself straying from the path. Just like anything in life, it's important to adopt a playful relationship, one in which you set the intention to engage the suggestions and practices and at the same time are also forgiving toward yourself when obstacles get in the way. So how do we persevere when life throws us its inevitable struggles?

Miriam was a seventy-two-year-old woman who exercised daily and was in excellent shape for her age. When asked what her secret was to waking up and exercising every morning, she said, "At some point I just understood that I needed to think of it just like I think about personal hygiene. I wake up every morning, and I brush my teeth and take a shower. I think of exercise the same way. Whenever I find myself not doing it, I forgive myself and just begin again."

This may be a good way of seeing how to approach this book—a sort of mental floss, a part of personal mental hygiene that we practice every day. There's a Buddhist saying: "If we are facing in the right direction, all we have to do is keep on walking." To this we might add, "Whenever we find ourselves off the trail, there's no need to entertain the hopeless critic; we can always wisely and compassionately begin again, putting one foot in front of the other."

You have already taken the first step—congratulations! As you continue facing in the direction you're intending to face, know you are not doing this only for yourself. Science shows us that our attitudes and behaviors have ripple effects across many degrees of people we know (Christakis and Fowler 2007). The intention and practice you put into *MBSR Every Day* is a gift not only to yourself but also to countless others.

Welcome to your journey of mindful living.

PART 1

One Moment

1

◆ ◆ ◆

Be a Beginner

Mindfulness-based stress reduction has made the raisin-eating practice famous. If you're not familiar with this, it is a practice in which you put on your creative and playful cap and imagine you are an alien from outer space who has just landed on this planet. On your travels, you come across an object—a raisin. Because you have never seen this object before, you carefully hold it and examine how it looks. You investigate the shape, color, contours, size, and perhaps even its translucent nature (if you happen to have come across a golden raisin). Then you continue through the senses. You feel the raisin, examining if it is rough or soft, warm or cool, wet or dry. Then you bring it up to your ear, roll it around and squeeze it a bit, noticing what you're hearing. Then to the nose, smelling once and then again. Finally, you've decided it is edible, and you place it in your mouth, noticing how the arm knows exactly where to go. As most people place it on their tongue, they notice their mouth is watering. They notice that the texture feels different to the tongue than it did to the fingers. As they bite down, a symphony of taste slowly spreads across particular areas of the tongue, until finally the last bit goes down the throat.

It's amazing what happens when we bring a beginner's mind to a simple experience like eating a raisin. Many people say things like, "I never knew a raisin could make sound," or "I never knew I could get so much satisfaction out of a single raisin." One elderly participant in a group exercise said, "My whole life I've been shoveling raisins down my mouth by the handful; this is amazing." He paused and then said, "It's only now that I realize…I don't even like raisins." Everyone broke out in laughter. How many things in life are we doing out of routine that we either don't enjoy or know aren't even good for us?

Japanese Zen priest Suzuki Roshi said, "In the beginner's mind there are many possibilities, in the expert's mind there are few." If the definition of mindfulness is "paying attention—on purpose and without judgment," then cultivating a beginner's mind is essential to mindfulness. With beginner's mind, we put aside our programmed biases of something being good or bad, right or wrong, fair or unfair. Instead, we engage with curious and fresh eyes—we eat a raisin for the first time. When we learn to bring a beginner's mind into our daily lives, the possibilities seem endless.

Just Do It!

Abraham Joshua Heschel said, "Life is routine and routine is resistance to wonder."

Beginner's mind is a practical approach to breaking free from old patterns and getting back in touch with the wonder of life. It's about being curious. You can practice it while eating food, looking at a tree or the sky, feeling the skin of a loved one, listening to birds, or smelling your favorite dessert.

Experience what beginner's mind feels like physically, emotionally, and mentally. In other words, how does the body feel when you take something in for the first time? What emotions arise? Does the mind seem distracted or clear?

Whatever it is, after doing this for a while, maybe a day or a week, reflect on what you noticed. Did anything surprise you?

2

♦ ♦ ♦

Come to Your Senses

One of the quickest ways to come down from a busy mind is to come to our senses—literally. Norman Farb and his colleagues (2010) found that when you bring your attention to the present moment, it slows activity in the part of the brain that is associated with a wandering mind. This makes sense. If you're sitting at a café and bringing awareness to your drink, you might notice the scent of it, its temperature, and how it tastes on your tongue. When you're fully immersed in that experience, it's unlikely you're worrying about what's coming tomorrow. But if you're drinking and worrying about tomorrow, you will probably finish the drink without tasting much of it.

We often take our senses for granted and don't recognize the gift of them until they fade or are gone. Maybe your vision begins to dull and you have to get glasses; or a ringing develops in your ears, and you lose your hearing. Maybe nerve damage makes it difficult for you to experience touch. Or it could be as simple as a common cold temporarily diminishing your sense of smell or taste. We don't have to wait for a catastrophe—or a cold—to begin bringing awareness to these gifts that are in the here and now.

You can begin cultivating mindfulness by bringing a beginner's mind to the magic of all your senses. Notice how alive you truly are.

Just Do It!

Right now take a moment of gratitude for all the senses that are working. Take a moment to bring a beginner's mind to each sense and be aware of it fully. Notice how your mind reacts to whatever it is you're sensing. Does it consider what you sense to be pleasant, unpleasant, or neutral? Become mindful of the world around you and inside of you.

- *Hearing*—Close your eyes and simply listen to the sounds around you. Notice how your mind jumps in to interpret and bring images to what it's hearing.

- *Seeing*—Take a look outside. Be amazed for a moment at how the eyes take in light rays and make sense of them. See all the colors and shapes. Notice what is moving and what is standing still.

- *Touching*—Maybe you feel called to close your eyes and feel your skin or perhaps the skin of a loved one (a human or a pet). Be aware of whether what you feel is smooth or rough, warm or cold, wet or dry. What do you notice?

- *Smelling*—Perhaps you want to take a walk into the kitchen, to a loved one, or around the block and open up to the world of smell. How does this feel in the body?

- *Tasting*—You can't forget this one. Find your favorite food or maybe just a snack. Bring a beginner's mind to it, like the previous raisin-eating meditation. If you find it to be good, spend a few moments lingering in that, choosing to savor what is good and noticing it as it fades away.

As you do this, shift your perception inside your body and note whatever you're feeling, physically and emotionally. After you finish, reflect on what it was like to bring a beginner's mind to your senses. Finally, thank yourself for taking the time to do this and consider the gift of having these senses at all. Try to bring awareness of your senses into every day, knowing how alive you truly are.

3

♦ ♦ ♦

Mind Your Thoughts

Years ago, the National Science Foundation said a person has about fifty thousand thoughts per day. Whether that is true or not, one thing you can be certain of is that the mind never stops thinking, analyzing, and trying to figure things out. It doesn't matter whether you're awake or asleep; the wheels keep turning. Our minds work just like a movie—in both images and words. Some of us think more often in images, while others experience more talking, and for some it's a good mix of both. The interesting thing is that most of the time, we're not even aware of what's going on in our minds.

When you begin to bring mindfulness to thoughts, one thing you notice is some kind of "self-talk" going on—you're talking to yourself. As we bring a beginner's mind to it, we can't help but notice how unbelievably hard we are on ourselves so much of the time. We say things that we would never say to a friend: *What is wrong with me?* or *I'm such an idiot* or *I'll never get this right.* Over time, we notice how mood distorts the thoughts in one direction or another. When we're in a good mood, the frequency and intensity of the negative thoughts lighten. Maybe we even notice ourselves thinking, *I'm brilliant!* And when there is more emotional distress, the negative thoughts become more intense and frequent.

But like all things, these mental formations have a life span, appearing and disappearing. Bringing mindfulness to our thoughts not only helps us become more familiar with the way our minds automatically operate but also frees us from having these thoughts dictate who we are and what we believe. You are not your thoughts—not even the ones that tell you that you are.

Just Do It!

From time to time today, ask yourself the simple question, *What is on my mind?* Do you notice that you are thinking mostly in images, words, or both? After being aware of one thought, ask yourself, *I wonder what thought will come up next?* Be curious about how your mind is so quick to judge yourself and other people. Do you notice how these various mind states—thoughts and images—are constantly changing?

Here are a few categories of thoughts that you may find your mind drifting into:

- *Catastrophizing*—This is the mind's "what if" game. It snowballs the worst-case scenario of the future with worried thoughts: *What if this happens? What if that happens?* These thoughts amplify anxiety and depression.

- *Blaming*—This is a mind trap in which some uncomfortable feeling is expelled by holding ourselves responsible for another's pain or holding others responsible for our pain. The problem here is that when you perceive the issue as lying outside of you, you give your power away to effect change.

- *Rehashing*—This is when our thoughts reflect on past circumstances, going over them again and again, often in an effort to figure something out.

- *Rehearsing*—This is the mind practicing some future event, playing through, again and again, the possible ways it may unfold.

Just intentionally being curious about how your mind works and even labeling certain categories of thoughts widens the space between awareness and the thoughts themselves. In that space is where your choice and freedom lie.

4

♦ ♦ ♦

Find Patience

There's a funny cartoon that has a group of monks gathered at what looks like a university campus. One monk stands on a bench with a megaphone in hand and asks, "What do we want?" The crowd responds, "Mindfulness!" The monk with the megaphone asks, "When do we want it?" and the crowd yells, "NOW!" While this is a play on mindfulness about being in the now, it also can be seen to represent our cultural drive toward impatience. It's not news that we grow up in a culture that wants everything now; this is why waiting is an intolerable activity for many people. Impatience is one of the greatest obstacles to developing mastery with anything.

When we're impatient, we're most apt to just give up. But one of the greatest skills we can develop—and one that will serve us along the travels of life—is *patience*.

Patience is that still voice inside that whispers *Slow down* and gives space to what's here. You begin to understand that this is the moment at hand, and that it's important to be present to it, since this moment is where life is being lived. Imagine if you had this voice within you when sitting in traffic, waiting in line at the grocery store, waiting for that girl you recently met to text back, or during one of your children's temper tantrums. What would be different? A whole lot less anxiety, and a whole lot more perspective and peace of mind. The wonderful thing about patience is that it's a skill that we can all learn, no matter our background or upbringing. The fact is that whether we're patient or impatient, the traffic is there, we're still waiting in line, the text still hasn't come, and our kid is still tantrumming. Who is suffering? You!

Patience is a strength that builds confidence and a sense of personal control. As you continue to bring *MBSR Every Day* into your life, there will be some things that come easily, while others will be more difficult. As best you can, remind yourself to practice patience. There is no mystery to this; what you practice and repeat in life becomes easier. Soon you'll find yourself getting better and better at living mindfully.

Just Do It!

The wonderful thing about practicing patience is that it turns all the moments of waiting in daily life—which we're often averse to—into opportunities for practice and growth. That's a pretty cool magic trick. Take a moment to think of all the times when you are impatient in your day.

Here's a list of ten common times of impatience:

- In traffic

- In line at the grocery store or ATM

- Downloading an app

- Listening to someone speaking while wanting to speak yourself

- Waiting for coffee or tea to brew

- Wanting a response from someone via text or e-mail

- When someone doesn't understand you

- Being with certain people

- While a child is throwing a temper tantrum

- Trying to fall asleep

As you start to recognize where impatience is in daily life, what you may find is that it's a felt experience in the body. Maybe it's a constriction in the chest or tension in the shoulders or face. You may also notice a sequence of reactive thoughts and emotions. You'll also notice that impatience has a life span; it naturally comes and goes, as all things do. If you just look around, you'll see that you're not the only one who struggles with being patient. The experience of not needing to be enslaved by impatience is empowering.

May we all grow in patience and experience the sense of freedom that has been there all along.

5

♦ ♦ ♦

Play!

When many of us look back at the time when we were kids, it wasn't chores and school that were most appealing; playtime was what we looked forward to the most. But something happens to us as adults—we are indoctrinated into a system in which play is relegated to the bottom of the priority list. It's not something we intentionally choose; it's a subtle process in which the belief is planted and nurtured that play simply isn't important, and as the years go on, we wonder why we "feel so old."

We don't stop playing because we grow old; we grow old because we stop playing.

This quote—by the Irish playwright George Bernard Shaw—hits the nail on the head. Youth is a matter of mind and attitude. One participant in our MBSR group was sixty-two years old, but he looked younger than that. He said, "My face reflects who I am on the inside." This is true; he is a playful guy—young at heart, as they say.

It has been said that by the time a person is fifty, he or she gets the face he or she deserves. This is how the mind directly affects the body. The truth is that we're never too old to start playing again. The question is, how can we bring more play into our lives?

Just Do It!

One of the wonderful things about mindfulness is that it encourages us to break out of routine and fall back into the wonder of daily life. Mindfulness and play go together. In the foreword to *A Mindfulness-Based Stress Reduction Workbook*, Jon Kabat-Zinn calls the practice of mindfulness a "playful adventure." The fact is that while there are so many benefits to living mindfully, we also can't take it too seriously. If we're too serious about staying present in our lives, then we become overly attached to mindfulness and become disappointed and frustrated when we're not present. Instead, we can bring that curious eye to mindfulness, and even in the moments when we're mindless (and there are plenty of opportunities there), we can say, *Ah, isn't that interesting—how did I get here?* This leads us to forgive ourselves for straying but also to learn how we got there. With this mindset, we come back to the beginning much sooner (wiring in a little happiness along the way).

Practice breaking out of routine and intentionally bringing play back into your life. In her book *The Artist's Way*, Julia Cameron suggests creating an "artist's date." All this means is that you take two hours a week to do something creative and fun that you would normally tell yourself that you don't have time to do. You can play the guitar, read poetry, sit in a coffee shop and write, go hiking in a new place, visit a new neighborhood, play video games, or start on that art piece you've been putting off because you "just don't have the time"—or because you're "not an artist."

Don't negotiate with your mind, which is telling you there's no time or that it's not important; just plan it and do it. We need to water the seeds of playfulness in our lives. This not only brings us more joy but also sets up a fundamental attitude that will serve our mindfulness practice. It is also what keeps our youth alive and likely elongates our lives. Give it a try!

6

♦ ♦ ♦

Be Mindful of a Simple Task

In life, there's a lot to do, and it seems like if we let it, life can become increasingly complex as responsibilities pile on. Sometimes it seems that there are so many balls in the air that it's impossible to keep juggling. Just in a single morning, after we wake up, we have to take a shower, make breakfast, eat breakfast, wash the dishes, and respond to e-mails and texts. If you're a parent, the list is longer: make everyone's lunches, make everyone's breakfast, wash the dishes, and get the kids dressed—all while trying to keep them from bouncing off the walls. That can be complicated.

When we start to understand that we can be mindful of simple tasks in life, things begin to change. Within our minds we hold the power to slow things down and be more intentional with our attention.

Not long ago I (Elisha) came home from seeing clients; all I wanted to do was rest. But we don't always get what we want. As life would have it, when I got home, my kids seemed like someone had spiked their juice with Red Bull, and my wife told me that she had a lot of work to do and asked if I would clean the kitchen after dinner. I bulldozed through the dishes, dreaming of a moment to relax downstairs.

As I walked downstairs, ready to collapse, I was surprised to find a giant pile of clean laundry waiting to be folded. Although I was immediately irritated, a moment of acceptance washed over me as I reset my expectations for the night and brought my attention to a single shirt in front of me. I picked it up, felt it in my hands, and gently folded it. I continued to do this, one piece at a time; there was something very soothing about it. I'd find some pieces that would bring up memories of my boys playing or a night my wife and I went out. As I did this, my whole body relaxed, and I found myself actually enjoying it. I was grateful for the reminder that mindfulness could be so powerful.

Just Do It!

As the fifteenth-century Indian poet Kabir said, "Wherever you are / is the entry point." The opportunity to drop into the present moment and be aware is always here. The morning shower is a great example, because many of us unintentionally use that time to plan for the day, thinking of all the to-dos ahead of us. All you have to do is bring in what you learned earlier in "Come to Your Senses" (chapter 2). Imagine this is the very first time you stepped into this shower. What do you see? Do you notice the water leaping off of your skin as it hits you? Do you see the shine or color of the soap or shampoo? What do you smell? Inhale once and then again. Feel your skin, your body, and whatever you feel drawn to. Is there a certain routine you have for the shower, and if so, what would happen if you shook it up a bit? Close your eyes and just listen to the rush of the water. Notice how it fluctuates. Be aware of what it's like to Be in the shower.

As you do this, check in with your body—how do you feel?

You can take this same practice and apply it to other simple tasks: walking, listening, eating, answering e-mails, being with your pet, being with your partner, gardening, or drinking a wonderful drink. When we're mindful of simple tasks in daily life, we turn down the volume of our wandering minds and open up to the aliveness that is all around us.

Take this opportunity; dip into the richness of your life.

7

◆   ◆   ◆

Connect

One of the pillars of mindfulness-based stress reduction is bringing mindfulness into ourselves and our relationships in daily life. As soon as we open our eyes in the morning, stories are running through our minds that influence the way we see people. We may have preconceptions about who our wife, husband, kid, roommate, or partner is. When we walk out the door, we may already have ideas about who the neighbors, baristas, grocery store clerks, colleagues, and even strangers are.

So the question is, do we actually even see the people behind our conceptions of who they are? Most of the time, the answer is a resounding no.

Mother Teresa said, "The biggest disease today is not leprosy or tuberculosis but rather the feeling of not belonging." We live on autopilot in our everyday relationships, and our ability to automatically interpret the world can lead to disconnection, which leads to *dis-ease* in life.

It's that simple.

The irony of living in the digital age is that while there are so many more ways of connection, many people are feeling more disconnected and alone. It's as if we've entered a trance in which our brains turn everyone into an object—and it's hard to connect with an object. But connection and a sense of belonging is always here; all we have to do is drop into it.

Just Do It!

Here is a practice to try today with anyone you come in contact with:

1. *Put your lenses of judgment aside*—Whether you believe it or not, we often judge someone as soon as we see him. It may be skin color,

ethnicity, a memory you have of this person, or maybe the expression on his face. See if you can set that aside for a moment and adopt fresh eyes.

2. *See the person*—This is someone who has a history of adventures, a sense of failure, loves, fears, regrets, triumphs, traumas, family, and friends.

3. *Ask yourself, what does this person most deeply want or long for?*—The answer is likely within you and it has something to do with being treated kindly and feeling a sense of belonging.

4. *Provide a gesture that feeds this need*—Smile at the person; ask her if you can help; listen to what she has to say; if the person is a friend or a family member, tell her you love her, and so forth. There are so many ways to do this.

The fact is that when we feel understood and cared about, a sense of acceptance and belonging arises. This breaks down barriers and simply makes relationships better. Like anything, this takes practice.

Just as a pebble thrown into the water creates ripples, a moment of mindful connection creates ripples of belonging wherever you go.

8

♦ ♦ ♦

The Gifts of Imperfection

You may have read the wonderful little story *Corduroy*. Corduroy was a teddy bear in a department store with a button missing on his overalls. Corduroy had an imperfection, and when a little girl came up to him and asked to buy him, her mom said, "Not today dear, we've already spent enough already and besides, he's missing a button." When they left, Corduroy was disturbed that he had this imperfection and went around the store on little adventures in search of his button. He never found it, but the next day the girl came back, bought Corduroy—imperfection and all—and gave him a home and a friend.

This is a famous book, read to millions of children (and parents). Why? Because it touches on a topic we can all identify with: the idea of being imperfect, but still deserving of love. We all feel vulnerable and have a button missing somewhere. We see it in being bald or overweight, or having wrinkles or a birthmark somewhere. Or maybe we feel inadequate as we struggle with anxiety, depression, obsessions, or addictive behaviors. At the heart of it, we all want to feel that we belong; we want a home and we want a friend.

To be in harmony with the wholeness of things is not to have anxiety over imperfections.

—Japanese Zen Buddhist teacher Dogen Zenji

Newsflash: to be imperfect is to be human. We might say, "We are all perfectly imperfect." Dropping anxiety about our imperfections doesn't mean becoming complacent about imperfections that might be harmful to our mental and physical health. We can still work to change them. It simply means understanding that we are all imperfect and beginning to practice kindness—instead of fear and hate—toward our imperfections. What would the days, weeks, and months ahead look like if we practiced more kindness toward our imperfections?

Just Do It!

Okay, let's get practical. How does this work in our daily lives? Think of it in three steps:

1. *Acknowledge imperfection*—The first step is to accept the fact that you are imperfect—as we all are.

2. *Notice judgments*—At any given moment, a negative thought may arise: *Yes, but I have many more imperfections than most people,* or *I'm just not following these practices right; I can't do this.* If this happens, recognize it as an automatic, habitual thought pattern (because that is what it is), let it be, and bring your attention to the third step.

3. *Re-parent with kindness*—Bring kindness to the moment. Bring your attention to the

feeling that is there right now. It is likely a physical feeling that is connected to an emotion—possibly an emotion of shame, disgust, fear, sadness, or anger. Put your hand where the feeling is and imagine it as a baby; maybe even imagine yourself as a baby or a little boy or girl. Now say to this part of yourself, "I care about your pain, and I love you just the way you are"—or use whatever words fit for you. You can do this for thirty seconds or thirty minutes—whatever feels right for you in the moment.

Every moment is an opportunity to hone mindfulness and self-compassion. Even now as you read this, there may be doubts or judgments in your mind, such as *This is lame,* or *I could never do this.* We all have automatic negative thoughts, and for many of us, they've been with us for a long time. The good news is their arrival gives us an opportunity to practice breaking free from them. This puts you back in the driver's seat and allows your experience—rather than the snap judgments—to be the teacher.

9

♦　♦　♦

Practice with Others

Since the dawn of human life, there has been a high value placed on community. All the world's wisdom traditions hold it as a pillar of living well. The people we surround ourselves with impact how we live our lives. If we spend most of our time with people who live in discord with our values, ultimately they will be depleting. If we spend time with people who live in accordance with our values, they will be supportive and nourishing. Finding people whom you can practice MBSR with will help you integrate it into your life and the lives of others.

The social scientists Nicholas Christakis and James Fowler conducted a study (2007) that shows the impact of our social networks. They examined the relationships of 12,067 people, who together had more than fifty thousand connections. Not only did they find that birds of a feather flock together, but they also found something far more interesting about our habits. For example, they found that obesity is "contagious" among friends up to three degrees of separation. In another study (Fowler and Christakis 2010), they found that loneliness and even happiness are also contagious up to three degrees of separation.

There hasn't been a study of it yet, but if many behavioral habits and emotions have been shown to be contagious up to three degrees, we can imagine that mindfulness is also contagious up to three degrees. Understanding the impact of our social connections and being intentional about whom we spend time with can make a big difference in integrating mindfulness into our lives.

Just Do It!

This isn't to say that you should throw away your friends who don't practice mindfulness. They may have their own nourishment they bring to your life.

We are saying, however, that you should discover people within your circle or outside your circle who are engaged in mindful living.

Here are five ways to start connecting now:

- *Start with your circle*—You might reach out to friends, family, or colleagues who may be interested in this.

- *Reach out to a wider MBSR community*— When we wrote *A Mindfulness-Based Stress Reduction Workbook*, we started a community online where members share their experiences. You can find it through http://www.mbsrworkbook.com. There are also many people who practice mindfulness around the globe; a good hub for MBSR communities is the Center for Mindfulness (CFM, http://www.umassmed.edu/cfm), where you can search for a local MBSR community.

- *Search out local groups*—Another wonderful resource to find local people who are practicing is http://www.meetup.com.

- *Find an online course*—If a local option isn't available, http://www.emindful.com hosts live online MBSR courses.

- *Visit a retreat*—You can also visit a retreat center, such as the Insight Meditation Society on the East Coast or Spirit Rock on the West Coast.

What is so fortunate today is that mindfulness is more mainstream than ever. This means that an increasing number of people are open to becoming more present to their lives. Take a moment right now or make a date with yourself later to explore one or more of these options to start building yourself a small community.

PART 2

Breathe

10

♦   ♦   ♦

Simply Breathe

Abraham Joshua Heschel was a rabbi and peace activist; he said, "Life is routine and routine is resistance to wonder." Our brains are so powerful that they can make seconds blend into minutes, which blend into hours, days, weeks, months, and years. One day, however, we wake up and wonder, *How did I get here?* Luckily, we have a portable and powerful resource that is with us at all times, inviting us to stop and just "be" with life instead of getting caught in the trap of "doing" so much.

This is our breath.

As we start to bring awareness to this fundamental process of being alive, we notice the mind's tendency to jump around quite a bit. We also notice how such a simple—though not always easy—practice of mindful breathing can quickly bring us back into the present moment and all the richness within it.

Throughout part 2, you'll be guided step by step into befriending the breath as a source of mindfulness in daily life. You'll learn how to prepare for practice, what posture is right for you, how to work with your "monkey mind," and even how to overcome one of the top obstacles: not having enough time to practice.

When we learn to trust in the breath, we begin to experience what all the scientific hype is about—how this simple practice can be an antidote for stress, anxiety, and restlessness, and how it can enlighten us to the nature of our minds and lead to states of insight and relaxation. Learning how to become intimate with our breath can widen the space between stimulus and response, which allows us to break from routine, open up to freedom, and choose to pay attention to the wonders all around us.

Just Do It!

No matter whether this is the first time you're bringing attention to the breath in this way or you've had a longstanding mindfulness practice, take a few seconds right now to bring a beginner's mind to your breathing. Where do you notice it most prominently? Is it at the tip of the nose, in the inner nostrils, the upper lip, the chest, the abdomen, or other places—or maybe it's a whole-body sensation? In this moment, does it seem shallow, deep, or somewhere in the middle? Do you notice a difference in temperature as you breathe in and breathe out?

In the following pages, we'll be preparing you for a breathing meditation, but for now we want to start this befriending process with something informal. Set the intention today to become aware of the breath from time to time. What do you notice about your breath while you're standing in line, stuck in traffic, at work, talking to your partner or a friend, or even as you're about to go to sleep?

What happens when you bring a curious attention to it? Is it pleasant, unpleasant, or neutral?

From time to time, allow life to be this simple.

11

♦ ♦ ♦

Prepare for Practice

There are many different ways that people can teach mindfulness, but in the way that we understand it, there are a few things that can help you enhance and deepen it right from the start.

Put on Your Learning Mindset

Before even attempting to do any practice, it's important to remember that your practice is not a performance. Each practice doesn't need to be evaluated about whether it was a "good" meditation or a "bad" meditation. This performance-based mindset misses the point entirely. If there is any goal at all to the practice, it's simply to open to what's directly here and learn.

Bring Heart into It

Mindfulness seems to be most effective when you bring your heart into it. Your awareness has a quality of relaxed curiosity, with tenderness. It's as if we're bowing with respect to the life being lived, whether the attention is on the breath, the body, or any sense perceptions.

When there is pain involved, there is an awareness of the pain, and the attention has a quality of wanting to be supportive in some way. It is a quality of care and self-compassion.

In other words, you're doing this practice ultimately because you care about yourself and possibly because you know that doing this practice will also be a gift to those around you.

Forgive Yourself

You're going to be completely imperfect at this—like the rest of us. If time goes by and you forget to practice, remember a practice called "forgive and invite." Forgive yourself for the time gone by, investigate what took you off course, and then, in that space of awareness, invite yourself to begin again.

Mindfulness is a very forgiving practice; you can always begin to be present to your life again. It only takes a moment. The moment you realize you're not present, you are—it is that close!

Thank Yourself

Perhaps the most important part of this practice is to thank yourself each time you do it. When the time is up, you acknowledge yourself for taking the time out of daily busy-ness for your own learning, health, and well-being.

This imprints in your memory that you care enough about yourself to pay attention to you. Such self-compassionate, caring energy is healing. What would the days, weeks, and months ahead be like if you had more of that energy circulating through your mind and body?

Just Do It!

As you go through the day today, see if you can apply any of these elements to things you are already doing. For example, if you're listening to a loved one, can you put judgments aside and have a *learning mindset*? What would it look like to *bring your heart into it* with a caring attention and even *be forgiving* of yourself if you don't say the right thing or if your attention strays? Finally, *thank yourself* for being so intentional with your life in that moment.

You can do this with any activity.

12

♦ ♦ ♦

Space, Time, and Posture

When it comes to setting time aside and starting a formal practice like the breathing meditation, it's important to consider where you're going to practice (Space), when you're going to practice (Time), and what position you will practice in (Posture). Understanding these three basics will give you a great foundation for the chapters that follow.

Space

You can be anywhere in the world—from the busiest streets of New York to a quiet cave in the Himalaya— and be aware of your breath. When you're starting out, however, it helps your concentration if you find a quiet space. Many people find it helpful to create a space at home as their meditation space—the bedroom, office, or living room. Or, if the outside is quiet enough, you could set it up on the balcony or porch or even by a tree. The main point is to find a place where you feel comfortable to come and sit daily.

Time

If there is any obstacle that gets in people's way of practice, it's having difficulty finding time. That is why it is so important to prepare for this from the get-go. Allow yourself to experiment with what the best time is for you to sit down and practice. Is it in the morning, during your lunch break, when you get home after work, or maybe at bedtime? You can also experiment with the length of time you want to practice. Start with five, ten, fifteen, or more minutes. Ultimately, what matters is that you make time—if you have time only to sit on the edge of your bed and take a few deep, conscious breaths before you go to sleep, that'll work. Give yourself some leeway to find out what time works best for you, and then commit to that time daily. Put it in your calendar as a priority meditation date with yourself.

Posture

The truth is that there is no one posture that is the "right" posture when it comes to practice. It is generally recommended to sit in a comfortable position on a cushion, chair, or meditation bench. In short, it can be any position in which you are comfortable and awake.

Cushion

You can buy a meditation cushion or fold a pillow and sit on the edge of it. A traditional posture is sitting with your legs crossed or with one leg folded in front of the other. You can also be in a full lotus position (both feet resting on your thighs) or a half lotus position (one foot resting on one thigh). It is helpful to have a fairly straight back—yet not too rigid—and make sure that the knees are lower than the hips. If you are unable to get your knees lower than your hips, and you'd still like to sit on a cushion, get a couple of blankets or pillows and place them under your knees for support. That way your back doesn't have to support them while you're sitting.

Bench

Another option is to use a meditation bench, which has a place to sit and a place for your legs underneath the bench. Many people find this comfortable, and the bench aligns you in a posture that makes it easy to keep your back straight.

Chair

If you choose a chair, having your feet flat on the floor will help you maintain a more alert posture and will allow your breathing to flow freely.

Ultimately, these are just suggestions; you will find what is most comfortable and effective for you as you play with the MBSR practices that follow.

Just Do It!

One thing that we've found invaluable in finding space and time is finding another person to practice with. Practicing with a buddy is not essential, but it really helps motivation. It also helps you feel more connected to others who are aligned with this interest of yours. See if you can think of anyone you know who might be willing to start this journey with you. Practicing it together not only helps you—it also might be just the gift your friend was looking for.

13

♦ ♦ ♦

Breath as an Anchor

Training the mind to be more aware of the breath can not only help you be grounded in moments of stress but also improve your focus and concentration at work and home. There is no particular way to breathe—the only instruction is to breathe normally and naturally. As the breath comes in, be aware of the breath coming in; as the breath goes out, be aware of the breath going out. It's that simple.

But don't be fooled—it's not that easy. The brain is always working, and there will be many distractions that are tempting to follow. You may also experience feelings of boredom, restlessness, or frustration that arise and jerk you away. Or maybe it's a sound that pulls at your attention.

Whenever you become aware of any of these "distractions," you are mindful. This is the moment when you can choose to come back again—and again. As you intentionally practice coming back into the present moment and noting and acknowledging wherever you went, little by little you are cultivating one of the core attitudes of MBSR—a sense of knowing and trusting in yourself. This is powerful.

You are learning that even though you may get distracted from time to time, you can always bring yourself back to your intention to be present to what matters. This type of training helps prime the pump of concentration by increasing your ability to sustain attention on the breath. Just as you may go to the gym and lift weights—and through this repetition, build muscle mass—work and repetition will strengthen your mind, making it easier to go back again and again to the breath. This will gradually bring you calmness and steadiness within your mind and body and will set up favorable conditions for deeper understanding to arise.

Just Do It!

Sit—right now—in a comfortable position (see chapter 12). Read the following instructions and then give this a shot. You can use a timer and set it for five to ten minutes or you can access the audio meditations that accompany this book, available at http://www.newharbinger.com/31731.

1. *Start with a mindful check-in*—It's often helpful to begin any formal practice by asking, *Where am I starting from right now?* Notice how you're feeling (physically) in this moment. Is there any tension or tightness you can ease? Also be aware of where you're starting this practice from emotionally. Are you stressed, anxious, restless, calm, or perhaps neutral? Does your mind seem busy from the start or do you notice it settling in?

2. *Be curious about your breath*—As you glide into the practice, be curious about where you notice the breath most prominently. Is it at the tip of the nose, in the nostrils, or in the rise and fall of the chest or abdomen? Or

maybe you notice breathing throughout your body. Wherever you notice it most prominently is where you're going to choose to focus your attention for this practice.

3. *Breathe*—Bring your attention to the area in which you notice your breath most prominently, and as you breathe in, just know that you're breathing in. If you can do this, recommit to doing it again on the outbreath. As you breathe out, just know that you're breathing out.

4. *Bring it back*—When the mind wanders to a thought, emotion, or sound, know that you are present and congratulate yourself, see where your mind went and then gently guide it back. It's not about how long you can stay on your breath; it's simply about bringing it back—again and again—training the brain to return and beginning to learn more about yourself and the workings of your mind and body.

5. *Repeat step 4 over and over.*

14

♦　♦　♦

Make Peace with Your Mind

A few years ago, Harvard psychologists Matthew Killingsworth and Dan Gilbert created an iPhone app called "Track Your Happiness," which measured how often our mind wandered from what mattered to us and what effect that had on our happiness. The app would ping participants throughout the day to find out if they were indeed paying attention to what they wanted to pay attention to, how happy they were, and other things. What they found was that people's minds wander about 46.9 percent of the time and that that was correlated with feeling unhappy (Killingsworth and Gilbert 2010).

In practicing breathing as an anchor (chapter 13), you may have noticed how easy it is for your mind to wander off. In fact, that's one of the top things MBSR participants notice about their minds when they start this practice. The wonderful news is that in this practice, a wandering mind will make an unhappy mind *only* if you attribute the wandering mind as something negative. Remember, the goal is not to focus on the breath for a long period of time; it's to learn what it's like to settle attention on the breath. If the mind wanders a lot, you learn how busy the mind is. If it wanders frequently onto a particular topic, you learn to what degree that topic is in your thoughts. If it is on your mind a lot, you learn that it needs attention, and you can later make the choice to focus on it.

Everyone's mind wanders—even for people who have been meditating for fifty years. It's part of what the mind does. In fact, you could make the argument that the more it wanders, the more you have an opportunity to train it to see "choice points" to gently bring it back. What you practice and repeat becomes a habit—so here, you're strengthening the habit of choice.

We suggest that you not try to make your mind wander less. This will save you a lot of suffering in the future. Mindfulness helps us learn how to dance with the mind and gain more confidence with it. While Killingsworth and Gilbert found that "a wandering mind is an unhappy mind," we'd argue that this isn't entirely true. It's more about how you relate to the wandering mind—this makes all the difference. When you relate to it with the attitudes and practice of mindfulness, you're not unhappy at all; you're practicing making peace with your mind.

Just Do It!

Set the intention for the days to come to notice when your mind is wandering from what it is intending to pay attention to. Maybe your intention is to answer a lot of e-mail at work, but you catch yourself daydreaming or off on social media sites. Or maybe your friend, partner, or child is talking to you, and instead of listening, you catch the mind drifting off onto the next great counterargument. Whenever you notice your mind wandering off, remember it is not "bad" that it wandered; it is a moment of awareness, a choice point to recognize where it went and gently guide it back.

With practice, you can get better and better at making peace with your mind.

15

♦ ♦ ♦

Uncover Gratitude

If you're breathing, you're alive and your body is working. The lungs are operating as they should be, bringing oxygen into the body, which gives you energy, helps digest your food, cleans out toxins, fuels muscles, and keeps the heart pumping. When you think about the breath in this way, every breath is a gift, and the awareness of breathing can give rise to the healing nature of gratitude.

How is gratitude healing? Robert Emmons and Michael McCullough (2003) conducted a study called "Counting Blessings versus Burdens." They split a group of people into three groups. One group counted five blessings per day, one group counted five burdens per day, and one group just wrote about neutral events. As you may have already guessed, the ones who counted their blessings experienced less stress and more feelings associated with well-being.

In every MBSR class we've taught—without exception—the experience of gratitude has arisen within the group. This is simply because we're finally coming home to ourselves. Even a simple breathing practice allows us to recognize the gifts in life that can free us from being constantly bogged down by the same routine. When we learn how to pause and pay attention to life itself, our eyes begin to open to the wonders that are often around us.

Just Do It!

Theologian, philosopher, and mystic Meister Eckhart said, "If the only prayer you said in your whole life was, 'thank you,' that would suffice." Whatever your experience with gratitude has been in the past, see if you can approach it right now with a beginner's mind, as if this was the first time.

Aside from coming to your senses (chapter 2), here we give you four ways to uncover gratitude right now.

1. *Bring gratitude into your breathing practice from time to time*—While practicing breath as an anchor, see if you can have the awareness that taking in oxygen allows you to be alive. Every breath is a source of nutrients that keep the body humming.

2. *Keep a gratitude journal*—It's possible you've heard this suggestion before, but ask yourself, when is the last time you tried it? This is the exact way that the participants in the "Blessings versus Burdens" study showed improvements in well-being. You can buy a journal to dedicate to this, or nowadays there are many apps that will help you keep this list. See if you can review it weekly, allowing it all to sink in.

3. *Remember when times were not so good*—This may seem a bit dismal, but it helps highlight what we have now that we may not have had in the past. Setting up this contrast can set the stage to inspire gratitude.

4. *Connect with people you are grateful for*—Whom in your life are you grateful for? What is it about them that inspires gratitude? Have you received something from them? Do they inspire you or support you physically or emotionally? Set the intention to connect with them more and have this in mind when you are with them. Ultimately, people are the best sources of gratitude.

Consider reading this chapter as planting a seed of gratitude within you. Water it regularly, and your garden will flourish.

16

♦ ♦ ♦

Trust Your Experience

Do you have any fear in this moment that you are suddenly going to stop breathing? Fortunately, our autonomic system takes care of this vital function. We can trust the breath to come in and go out. If we had to take the reins for breathing, we probably wouldn't have survived as a species. Trust is a wonderful attitude to cultivate. It helps us feel safe and secure, which ultimately is the foundation for feeling happy.

Trust starts with us.

As we begin to dip into the practice of mindful breathing, we are essentially cultivating intimacy with ourselves. There's a sense of coming home. We can open up to a wider awareness of trust—how we trust our heart to pump, our lungs to process oxygen, and perhaps our eyes to see and ears to hear. We trust in the changing seasons.

But when it comes to trusting ourselves, the brain needs memories of experiences when the breath helped us open up to something beautiful or helped us rely on ourselves to handle a difficult situation. The more we intentionally practice and repeat using the breath as an anchor in daily life, the more memories are stored that can be retrieved in the times that follow. This is how we can use our minds to create a more trusting brain.

But like anything, it takes intention, attention, and practice.

Unfortunately, just sitting with yourself for five, ten, or fifteen minutes (or more) and paying attention to your breath is—for many of us—an act of being vulnerable. The fact is that throughout the day, most of us are guarding against being alone by either staying busy in activity or staying busy in our minds. But in paying attention to the breath, you build trust that you can actually be with yourself— with whatever is here. Through practice and repetition, the brain changes, and a new thought can emerge from the neural growth that says, *I can handle this; it's going to be okay.*

The fact is that we are active participants in our health and well-being; we all have a hand in learning how to shape our brains to trust ourselves.

It starts right now—and whenever we stray off the path, we can always begin again.

Just Do It!

Learning to trust ourselves is essential for our happiness. In addition to continuing mindful breathing, there are a number of ways you can begin practicing building self-trust in daily life. One way is to just lie down, in whatever position you think of as comfortable or cozy, on your couch or bed. Get as comfortable as you can. Then ask yourself, *How do I know that I am comfortable?* As silly as this question may seem, the answer reinforces that you can trust your experience.

Take this concept out into the world, and if there is an uncomfortable moment, whether physically or emotionally, ask yourself that same question: *How do I know if this is comfortable or uncomfortable?*

As you do this, you're creating memories in which your experience matches what is happening. This reinforces self-trust.

If you stay there with the feeling, what you will eventually find is that the comfort or discomfort doesn't ever stay the same. We can't hold on to any particular experience, as the nature of things is to come and go. That's a natural law—notice the freedom that arises as you begin to trust in the impermanence of life.

PART 3

Tune the Heart

17

♦ ♦ ♦

Practice "Kindfulness"

In many Asian languages, the word for "mind" and the word for "heart" are the same word. When we hear the word "mindfulness," it's important to understand that implicit in it is a soft, kind, and warm attention. We're paying attention in this way because we deeply care about ourselves, the people around us, or—for some—even the world. Therefore, the quality of heart is implicit in this work. We don't have to search for it; it's already here.

If you've ever taken an MBSR class, you know that the act of kindness to ourselves or others is caught all the time. It's caught in the moments when people recognize they're struggling and let it be instead of fighting it. It's caught when participants find the self-critic highly active, and layer in a quality of gentleness. It's caught when someone begins to recognize that there is a common humanity behind all our joys and sorrows. In one of our classes, a student said, "It's almost like mindfulness should maybe be called 'kindfulness,' because it's such a kind way of living." From that point on, the term "kindfulness" really stuck with us. When we intentionally cultivate loving states of awareness, we inevitably find that there is far more that bonds us than divides us, and we feel more connected.

As you deepen your experience with mindful presence, you can tune the quality of heartfulness, thereby deepening the essential nuance of love that is embedded in mindful living. After all, science shows that kindness toward others in need can provide a buffer against stress (Poulin et al. 2013), and kindness toward ourselves increases well-being (Neff and Germer 2013). The attitude of kindness is inherent in a meaningful life, and it has also been found to be associated with reduced cellular inflammation, which is at the root of disease (Fredrickson et al. 2013).

The Dalai Lama says, "My religion is kindness." What would the days, weeks, and months ahead be like if we all tried to be a little kinder?

Just Do It!

We can do small things to tune our hearts. Think of someone right now who is easy to love. This could be a person or an animal. Picture this person during her happiest moments of life. Reflect on what it is about her that you love so much. Consider what it is that you want for her. Maybe it's to be happy, to be healthy, and to feel deeply loved. Look at a picture of her or visualize her in your mind and say, "May you be happy, be healthy, and feel deeply loved." Or if you're feeling particularly courageous, drop her a text, e-mail, or phone call—or go visit her in person—and say this to her directly.

Allow yourself to linger in this intentional practice of tuning your heart.

18

♦ ♦ ♦

Love Yourself

When Julia walked into our class, she wore her stress on her sleeve. She was working fifty hours a week at an insurance company and doing her best to have a healthy marriage, all while mothering three children. She found herself in a constant swirl of to-dos, with frequent intrusive thoughts that she was "not good enough." When she was instructed to bring a kind attention to her experience, a loud voice inside erupted: "NO!"

Lack of self-kindness may just be the great unnamed epidemic of our time. We grow up in a culture that sees self-kindness as self-indulgent or a form of narcissism. The reality is, however, that it's one of the most practical ways to bring us into a state of mental health (and the world into global health). Consider if you were wounded on the side of the road—what would you need? You would first need to acknowledge the wound and then inspect it. Then you would care for yourself as you carefully cleaned the wound, applied a healing agent, and then bandaged it to protect it. Why should our emotional lives be any different?

If you were stranded on an island for the rest of your life and had to choose one person to be with, wouldn't you want someone you knew to be kind? It turns out that while some of us have more of a disposition to kindness than others, it's a skill that any of us can build (Neff 2011). Even with ourselves, we can nurture the quality of kindness as we begin to befriend our own souls. Every time we bring the intimate quality of "kindfulness" to ourselves, we are sowing the seeds of self-love, which is the greatest healer of all.

As for Julia, with a bit of patience and persistence, self-kindness finally began to settle in, and toward the end of the program she said, with tears brimming from her eyes, "I finally heard that small voice inside say, 'I love you,' and I believed it."

Just Do It!

The fact is that you are the owner of your actions and an active participant in your own health and well-being. Why not take the leap into loving yourself, even if it's only to be 10 percent kinder for now? Life will always present us with stressors, annoyances, and uncomfortable challenges. Take a moment to reflect on a recent difficult experience. What was it that you needed in that moment? Was it to have strength, to feel safe, or to have more peace? What do you notice if you start to send these intentions inward: *May I be strong, feel safe, be at peace?* Do you notice an aversion similar to what Julia noticed at the beginning of the class—or maybe it feels soothing?

Continue to play with the practice of being your own best friend. What's the risk? Might you reduce the pileup of frustrations and resentments and instead build more ease, safety, and freedom? Instead of doing random acts of kindness, with a little intention, we can create radical acts of kindness.

19

◆　◆　◆

Open Up to Joy

Opening up to joy for ourselves and others is essential to balance our brains. However, for better *and* worse, we are endowed with a brain that is inherently biased to pay more attention to negative than to positive stimuli (Ito et al. 1998). If you were walking in a field and you saw a lion on one side and a majestic waterfall on the other, which would you pay attention to? No matter how majestic the waterfall is, we are wired to survive in order to pass our genes on to the next generation. That means that all your negative thoughts are stickier than the positive ones.

But wait, there's even more bad news. Many of us are also wired to be suspicious of joy. The brain thinks that if we are too happy or joyful, we may be caught off guard by potential threats. Also, some of us grew up in a culture that taught us that opening up to our own joy and achievements seemed narcissistic or indulgent. Therefore, we may be quick to move on from joyful moments. Brené Brown (2012) has called this experience "foreboding joy." With mindfulness, we can help the brain evolve to feel less stressed *and* more open to the joy that's inherent in our lives and the lives of others. This act of "kindfulness" awakens the heart.

Just Do It!

The following is a practice with the intention of stirring up an awareness of joy—and perhaps of the obstacles that get in the way.

Have Joy for Your Joy

Play with the following phrases and see what arises within you.

- *"May I enjoy the achievements of my life."*
- *"May I open to the joy that is in me, and be happy."*

- *"Breathing in, opening to joy, breathing out, I smile."*

If you notice judgments about this being silly or self-indulgent, stay with it anyway, and allow your experience to guide you, not your judgments.

Have Joy for Another's Joy

Think of someone in your life whom you really care for. Picture this person or animal, and then say to yourself:

- *"May I open to the joy in you."*
- *"May I delight in your success and be happy for it."*
- *"May your happiness and good fortune not leave you."*

Remember, the only intention here is to incline your mind toward your heart. Notice whatever arises physically, emotionally, and mentally as you do this.

Have Joy for All Our Joy

Finally, open this to all people (and also hear us saying this to you, if you can take it in):

- *"May all people enjoy success in whatever they set out to do."*

- *"May we all be free of jealousy and envy of others."*
- *"May everyone who has good fortune share their good fortune with others."*

Know that as you move through your life, there is nobody more deserving of kindness and joy than you. Your brain's guarding against joy is not your fault—it's just the way it is, so it's important to be intentional in tuning a mindful heart.

See if you can plant the seeds of intention to be aware of joy. When it's there, ask yourself, *In this moment, can I feel joy for my joy?* See what follows.

20

◆ ◆ ◆

Smile (It's Good for You)

The powerful lessons that come from MBSR are far too serious to take seriously. We need to make sure these experiences are balanced with some lightness and humor. The Dalai Lama often speaks of the power of humor and smiling not only to tune our hearts but also to bridge a connection between people, even between enemies. Science has shown that smiling—especially the kind of smile that involves the muscles around the eyes—creates a specific type of brain activation that's connected to being in a kinder and happier mood (Ekman, Davidson, and Friesen 1990). Recent research shows that this kind of smile, known as a "Duchenne smile," leads to lower heart-rate levels and quicker recovery from stressful activities (Kraft and Pressman 2012).

Sometimes when we're practicing mindfulness, it's almost as if the quality of attention we need is a smiling heart. It's the kind of smile you might give to a newborn baby, who is so fragile and vulnerable. We want to direct this type of warm and kind attention inward. This isn't always so easy, however, so at first we may practice it more often on the outside. Over time, it can get easier to fine-tune the quality of "kindfulness" on the inside.

And it turns out that practicing being mindful of smiling and humor in daily life may have an even greater benefit than tuning our individual hearts. Smiling and laughter are contagious! If you doubt it, go to YouTube and look up "Laughter Attack at a Bus Stand" (there are a number of videos of laughter attacks). The Vietnamese Buddhist monk and activist Thich Nhat Hanh says, "Sometimes your joy is the source of your smile, but sometimes your smile can be the source of your joy."

Set any judgments aside for right now and ask yourself, what would your life be like if there was more smiling and laughter in it? What would the world be like if there was a bit more smiling and laughter? Would the world be a happier and even kinder place?

Just Do It!

It takes seventeen muscles to smile and forty-three to frown. It takes approximately two hundred thousand frowns to create one permanent frown line on your forehead. Thus a smile helps you look better and younger. Experiment with being more intentional about smiling today. Do this with your local grocery clerk, your neighbors, friends, or the person walking by you on the street. Feel free to laugh in public—it turns out it's an altruistic act. If you need a little help, look up "Benefits of Laughter Yoga with John Cleese" on YouTube, press play, and see what you notice.

Why not start bringing mindfulness to smiling right now?

21

♦　♦　♦

Be Generous

Henry David Thoreau said, "Goodness is the only investment that never fails."

Hilde Back was the daughter of Holocaust survivors and felt a tugging need to be generous and help others who were suffering. She decided to reach out to a young Kenyan student through an education charity. She sponsored a student named Chris Mburu and sent him a little money every month so he could continue his education.

This act of generosity changed Chris's life forever. He loved education; he went on to graduate from Harvard Law School and became a human rights lawyer for the United Nations. He then went on to create the Hilde Back Education Fund to offer rural Kenyan children a life of possibility.

Hilde's generosity caused ripple effects across more lives than she could have imagined.

Generosity is a fundamental quality of MBSR, just as patience, letting be, and gratitude are. The intention of giving can be used as a way to tune the heart, and it can be an exercise inclining toward a practice of generosity. The best place to start may be with yourself. We often feel guilty about accepting kindness, feeling we somehow don't deserve it. Practicing generosity with yourself helps you feel "good enough" to accept kindness from yourself without guilt. Set any judgments aside and notice what it's like to simply receive. If you notice the judgment that this seems self-indulgent, be curious about that—why would it be indulgent to love yourself? Who else benefits when you love yourself? What might be the gifts?

After you put on your proverbial oxygen mask, consider how to nurture the heart in being generous with others. It turns out that, like smiling and laughter, being generous is a contagious act. Giving causes others to give as well. Social scientists James Fowler and Nicholas Christakis (2010) have shown that inclining your heart toward others is contagious. Think of the news reports of people paying for the coffee of the person behind them at a drive-thru and how those coffee drinkers paid it forward. These generous behaviors lasted for hours. Fowler and Christakis also found that when the people around us are happy, we also become happier.

Just Do It!

Consider this right now: How can you nurture the essential attitude of generosity?

- What are some ways you are generous to yourself? Maybe even taking the time to engage this book for your own learning, health, and well-being is an act of being generous.

- With others, could you carry some petty cash with you to give to people you see who are in need? If you don't want to give money, could you buy them some food?

- Could you provide a smile a bit more often to the people you interact with from day to day?

- What about being more intentional about deeply listening to another person, listening with your heart and mind?

The best way to prime your mind toward generosity is to practice asking, *How can I give?*

Now make a plan and *just do it!*

22

♦ ♦ ♦

Remember to Forgive

Forgiveness is another essential attitude of mindfulness that can help cultivate greater understanding, ease, and freedom. It has been shown to reduce stress, anger, and depression and to support many aspects of well-being and happiness. Try a little experiment. Think of someone in your life right now who has slighted you in some way (maybe not the most extreme slight) and for whom you are holding some bitterness. Picture that person and hold on to that unwillingness to forgive. Now, just observe any emotions you have: anger, resentment, fear, sadness. Also notice how you are holding your body—is it tense anywhere or feeling heavy? Now bring awareness to your thoughts—are they hateful and spiteful thoughts?

Pause before continuing to read. Just take in this experiment.

Most people we do this with find it to be an uncomfortable experiment. It elicits feelings of tension and anger and thoughts of ill will toward the other person. The experiment doesn't conjure these feelings out of nowhere; it just brings to light what is already within us, stirring around. There is a common misconception that forgiveness means condoning the act of the other person. Forgiveness simply means releasing this cycle of torture that continues to reside inside.

It's heartfelt and courageous to say, *I have been offended against. I am going to let go of this so I don't continue to be burdened by it.* You have already been hurt once; why continue letting it torment you by holding on to it, with the erroneous belief that doing so is somehow getting back at the other person? When we hold a grudge, a "grievance story" builds in the mind, and as we hold on to it, we continue to fuel it, sowing the seeds of our own suffering.

Forgiveness is the practice of learning how to let go of this story in the service of loving ourselves.

Just Do It!

Right now we're going to give you a way to loosen the grip of grudges and tune a mindful heart. As you go through these steps, remember that your intention is to nurture peace within yourself, not assuage any other party.

1. *Articulate it*—Think about someone you hold bitterness toward and articulate why what this person did was not okay to you.

2. *Get perspective*—Recognize that your primary distress is coming from the hurt feelings, thoughts, and physical upset you are suffering now, not what offended you or hurt you two minutes—or ten years—ago.

3. *Make a choice*—Decide if you're ready to let go of this burden.

4. *See who is suffering*—Instead of mentally replaying your hurt from long ago, see if it's possible to recognize that you are suffering now and ask yourself, *What is it that I really need?* Is it to feel safe, to be understood, to be loved, to be free? If possible, contact the person to make amends; if that's not possible, seek out new ways to get what you want.

5. *Practice kindfulness*—Instead of focusing on your wounded feelings and thereby giving the person who caused you pain power over you, learn to look for the love, beauty, and kindness around you. Forgiveness is about personal power.

Amend your grievance story to remind yourself of the heroic choice to forgive.

23

♦ ♦ ♦

Be Gentle

Mahatma Gandhi said, "In a gentle way, you can shake the world." A central thread that moves through all the practices of MBSR is the attitude of gentleness. In fact, another way to define "mindfulness" may be "intentionally paying attention in a *gentle* way, while putting aside our programmed biases." The practice of being gentle with ourselves is a way of softening the heart. Even as we move through a simple breathing practice, you'll hear the instruction, "When you notice your mind wandering, just note that you are thinking and *gently* guide awareness back to the breath." This gentleness is intentional. We want to give our brains the experience of being consciously gentle over and over again, so that it's more likely to occur automatically in daily life.

Usually when people enter an MBSR program, there is a tendency toward being self-critical, or if they're experiencing an uncomfortable emotion, they're inclined to suppress that emotion. There's a tendency toward *care-lessness*. Being gentle in life implies a 180-degree shift to a practice of doing things with care. When we're picking up a newborn, carrying a hot cup of tea, or transferring a tender plant into a new pot, we're gentle. If you think about it, we're often gentle with things that are precious and delicate. Life itself is precious and delicate.

Paradoxically, it is often the unpleasant experiences in life that give us the greatest opportunity to practice the essential energy of gentleness. The energy of mindfulness is like a parent or older sibling holding a baby in her arms; there's a sense of tenderness in taking care of this child. Mindfulness holds uncomfortable feelings gently, as if they were a baby. While doing a breathing practice, a participant in one of our classes said that during the meditation she felt a great deal of restlessness. We asked, "Did you notice where you felt that in the body?" She considered the question and said, "Yes, it was a tightness in my shoulders," and she went on to say the tightness was still lingering there and was uncomfortable. The class paused as we asked her, "Is it possible, just for a few moments, to hold this restlessness as you might a baby, with gentleness and care?" She took a moment and allowed for this experience to settle in. In a few moments, she took a deep breath and said it had softened.

To be gentle is to be powerful.

Just Do It!

We can get better and better at being gentle with ourselves by simply practicing it in daily life. Try spending a portion of the day walking gently in your office, or take your shoes off and do so upon the earth. How would it feel to be gentler as you cook a meal today or even eat a meal more gently? Can you see how the child is always alive in you, and when an unpleasant emotion arises within the days that follow, can you inquire if it may need gentleness instead of self-judgment? As you practice gentleness, see if this attitude starts coming to you naturally, like moments of grace throughout the day.

May you go gently in the days to come.

24

♦ ♦ ♦

Open Your Heart to Others

Every day we look at ourselves in the mirror, but we don't actually see the person that is there. We are more likely looking to see if our face or body looks presentable. Every day we do the same with other people—at home, at the office, and on the street. Our brain chunks people into objects, categorizes them, and defaults to not really seeing the person who is there. After all, there are more urgent things to pay attention to moment to moment, like the next message on our phones. The fact is, however, that whether it's yourself in the mirror, a loved one, or a stranger, you may never see that person again, and every moment gives you an opportunity to see the uniqueness of the human being in front of you.

What would it be like to set an intention to take some mindful moments with yourself or the people in your life and behold the beauty and mystery of another human being? Everybody you see in any given moment has gifts and strengths that they might not even be aware of. Behind the eyes of every person is a deep well of courage and intelligence, patience, generosity, and even wisdom. Each person is likely far more powerful than he or she even knows. Take some moments to look into one man's eyes; he was once a child, and that child is still within him. Imagine the woman in front of you as your own child; see the beauty that is there. Consider how you would want her to bring her beauty into the world. What would you wish for them? Maybe your heart says you want them to be happy, to be healthy, or to be free.

Mindfulness facilitates the experience of connection with ourselves and with others. It's an experience of coming home.

Just Do It!

Play with this as a practice today with yourself and others. See if you catch the experience of kindfulness.

PART 4

Meditate

25

♦   ♦   ♦

Start with Your Body

In the first three parts of *MBSR Every Day*, you've learned many informal ways of bringing MBSR into your life. This has prepared you for a mindfulness meditation practice. The formal practice of MBSR is about intentionally setting time aside to engage in a mindfulness meditation practice. Here in part 4, you'll learn the fundamental mindfulness meditations that lie within MBSR, how to work with the inevitable challenges that arise in doing those meditations, and the mental attitudes necessary to make your practice come alive. In MBSR, the first formal practice starts with the body.

From the moment of conception, genetic instructions unfold to build the body you are using to hold this book and read these words. A number of elements come together—oxygen, carbon, hydrogen, nitrogen, calcium, and phosphorus—to make up the thirty-seven trillion cells in your body. If you lined up all these cells, you would circle the earth more than two times. These cells all have jobs that keep us functioning and healthy. Some carry oxygen to parts of the body in need; others are programmed to defend against intruding bacteria and viruses. Then there are the cells that transmit information—as you read these words, cells are bringing the information from your eyes to your brain. All of these cells that make up this body are tirelessly working for us, but how often do we pause and tune into the wonder of this body?

When we have a toothache, we know that not having a toothache is a wonderful thing. But when we do not have a toothache, we are still not happy. A non-toothache is very pleasant. There are so many things that are enjoyable, but when we don't practice mindfulness, we don't appreciate them.

—Thich Nhat Hanh

If our body is doing well, we don't notice it. Mindfulness gives us a way to practice attuning to the body and using it as a barometer for how we're feeling. Even more, as we bring mindfulness to the body, it inevitably unveils the secrets to a life of greater calm, contentment, and confidence.

Just Do It!

Practice a body-scan meditation. Find a space on the floor to comfortably lie down. If you are particularly tired or suffer from chronic pain and lying down is uncomfortable, you are welcome to sit in a chair or find another comfortable posture. You can practice this for five, ten, fifteen, or thirty minutes (or more). Try doing it daily for at least a week. It may help to review "Prepare for Practice" (chapter 11) prior to doing the body scan. (Note: You can find an audio download of this practice at http://www.newharbinger.com/31731.)

The steps of this body scan are fairly simple.

1. *Mindful check-in*—Start off with a short mindful check-in, sensing where you're starting from in this moment physically, emotionally, and mentally.

2. *Breath as an anchor*—Begin to become aware of your body just naturally breathing. See if you can rest your attention on this natural rhythm of being alive. If it helps, say *In* in your mind as you breathe in and *Out* as you breathe out.

3. *Toes to head*—Bring a beginner's mind to this practice and be mindful of whatever you're feeling physically, mentally, and emotionally. Start with your feet and notice sensations on all parts of the foot—the toes, soles, the tops of your feet, and even the ankle joints. Whatever you sense there, feel into it as it ripples and resonates wherever it needs to go. As you go through each part of

the body, you might even consider how each part allows you to function in the world, inspiring an appreciative awareness. In the torso, you have the heart, stomach, and lungs, allowing for circulation, digestion, and respiration. Have an awareness of that too. Continue to do this all the way up the body until you get to the top of the head.

4. *Breathe*—After you go through the body, narrow your attention back to the breath. Notice how with an inhalation, the whole body slightly expands, and with an exhalation, it contracts. Feel into the wholeness of the body.

5. *Acknowledge yourself*—Finally, acknowledge the choice you made to engage in this practice for your own health and well-being. This is an act of self-care.

26

♦　♦　♦

Know These Five Obstacles

When I (Elisha) first started practicing mindfulness meditation, I noticed a lot of resistance to practice. I was restless trying to be still, irritated when I couldn't focus, uncertain how it was going to benefit me, almost drifting off to sleep at times, and often just wanting to be doing something other than meditating. I didn't realize it at the time, but I had nailed some of the key obstacles to practice that people have been talking about for thousands of years. Understanding these obstacles and learning to be curious about them not only continues to help me work with them in my practice but also—perhaps paradoxically—awakens me to greater clarity and balance in my practice and life in general. As you read the following five hindrances, see which ones you recognize in your meditation practice and also in daily life.

1. *Wanting*—The mind hardly ever seems to be satisfied; it's always craving something. Before you start practicing, your mind may want the conditions to be different than they are—sometimes you want this so badly you never manage to start practicing. Or maybe as you start practicing, the mind wanders off onto your favorite food and fantasizes about eating it. This state of mind can stop us from practicing, distract us in practice, or ignite restlessness.

2. *Irritation and aversion*—If you don't feel that you're having a "good" meditation experience—or if there's an annoying noise in the room—it's easy to feel irritated. Irritation left unchecked can make us want to give up.

3. *Sleepiness*—Many of us are tired because we don't get adequate sleep, so it's easy to feel a bit sleepy when we come down from our busy minds. Our body does what it naturally wants to do: go to rest. We can also feel sleepy when an experience is overwhelming, so it's good to be curious whether the tiredness is telling you that you need more rest or that there's a feeling that needs to be expressed.

4. *Restlessness*—If you've started practicing, you may have noticed that it can be hard to be still for a period of time; the mind can be so busy. We're trained from a young age to do, do, and do some more. The mind may rebel a bit when learning how to "be." You might catch it running through a million to-do lists or trying to count the minutes until the end of the practice. This is all completely natural.

5. *Doubt*—The uncertainty about whether something will "work" often plagues people

in the beginning of their practice. They think, *This can work for others, but it won't work for me.* Doubt becomes a problem when it hijacks an initial action and the ability to allow experience to be our guide.

Just Do It!

The fact is that if you can recognize it, you can face it, and if you can face it, you can work with it; and as you do, the gifts will arise. For now, the instruction is simple: choose the obstacle that gets in your way the most and practice noticing it this week. For example, if you experience restlessness, see if you can notice when it's there; become curious about how it expresses itself in the body. You can do this with any of the obstacles. When you're ready, gently redirect your attention back to the practice. You can also take this "off the cushion" and notice when any of these obstacles arise in daily life. Be forgiving of yourself and remember that as you stray, you can always begin again.

27

♦ ♦ ♦

Apply These Five Antidotes

On the one hand, simply being aware of the five obstacles to practice—naming them and being curious about them—is a powerful practice. On the other hand, mindfulness affords us the awareness and choice to apply certain actions that can serve as antidotes and opportunities for growth. When you become mindful, you have the ability to step out of the old, reactive patterns that are fueled by unawareness and choose a more constructive response.

Antidote for wanting: curiosity and contentment—A craving generally has a shelf life of twenty minutes or less. If you notice you're wandering off onto something you desire, practice acknowledging how you're feeling in the body and mind. Become curious about what it is that you are longing for. Remind yourself that contentment can also be found in the here and now. Be mindful of this craving arising and then watch it slowly pass; feel the contentment that arises when you are free of wanting. We can inspire contentment with practicing being at ease with the way things are.

Antidote for irritation and aversion: mindfulness and self-compassion—While our urge may naturally be to resist any irritation that comes, we have to remember the adage "what we resist persists." The work here is to include irritation as part of the mindful experience. What happens when we allow the irritation to just be? Can you apply some self-compassion? Say to yourself, *May I be at ease*. See what you notice.

Antidote for sleepiness: concentration and self-compassion—If you occasionally fall asleep when meditating, consider it a good nap that you needed. If this is happening often, however, you might try sitting in a more upright posture, standing up, having your eyes slightly open, or maybe splashing some water on your face before starting. You can even shift into a walking meditation. If you're really daring, see what it's like to be curious about the feeling of sleepiness; open your eyes and experience the sensations of tiredness as they are. Do they stay? Do they come and go?

Antidote for restlessness: mindfulness—It's important to recognize that restlessness and boredom are just sensations, like any other. Try adopting a beginner's mind and being curious about the sensation of restlessness. As you do this, you may notice how the feeling of it has a life of its own, shifting and changing, arising and passing away. As you recognize restlessness, you can gently bring your attention back to the point of focus; see if the restlessness can become a teaching about the nature of change.

Antidote for doubt: mindfulness—Doubt is natural. One way to take control of it is to actively investigate it. Does the doubt reactively keep you away from experiencing the practice? Clarify what the value of the practice is to you; make a list of its benefits. We have to remember that thoughts are just thoughts; they're not facts (even the ones that say they are). If you notice doubt slipping into your practice, just take note of it and ask yourself, *Is this doubt absolutely true?* Follow that with, *What would be different if this doubt wasn't here?* Ultimately, the goal of mindfulness meditation is to allow your experience—not the reactive judgments—to be your teacher, inspiring clarity.

Applying the antidotes to each of these obstacles not only deepens our sense of freedom from the mind's reactivity but also gives us the opportunity to strengthen key factors of well-being. We begin to train mindfulness with flexibility, clarity of mind, and compassion, and we feel more confident in our ability to make wise choices. This internal sense of control breeds confidence and joy.

Just Do It!

Whatever the obstacles are that you recognize in your practice, begin applying the antidotes to them. If irritation is a common experience, notice what happens when you see it as an opportunity to strengthen mindfulness. Bring a beginner's mind to the sensation of irritation, feeling it as it comes and goes. You can also recognize the struggle of it and water the seeds of a kind heart, saying to yourself, *May I be at ease.* Choose the obstacle that seems to appear most often and play with the antidote each time it appears.

In doing this, we transform obstacles into opportunities for learning and growth.

28

◆　◆　◆

Welcome and Entertain Them All

Deep in the human brain lies a small structure the size and shape of an almond called the amygdala. The function of the amygdala is to assign emotional meanings to the stimuli we receive from the outside world. The amygdala classifies stimuli as something we should approach or avoid. This amygdala response thrusts us into a moment of anxiety, joy, sadness, shame, or anger, among other emotions. These emotions are energy that's experienced in the body. They can be uncomfortable, comfortable, or neutral. But no matter what emotion it is, it's always "in motion." In his wonderful book *The Essential Rumi*, Coleman Barks translates a poem by Rumi

that shows us the kind of attitude we want to hold
toward our feelings.

> This being human is a guest house.
> Every morning a new arrival.
> A joy, a depression, a meanness,
> some momentary awareness comes
> as an unexpected visitor.
> Welcome and entertain them all!
> Even if they are a crowd of sorrows,
> who violently sweep your house
> empty of its furniture,
> still, treat each guest honorably.
> He may be clearing you out
> for some new delight.
> The dark thought, the shame, the malice,
> meet them at the door laughing and invite them in.
> Be grateful for whatever comes,
> because each has been sent
> as a guide from beyond.

How we're feeling emotionally influences our
moment-to-moment perception of life. When we're
in a good mood, we see a situation one way; when
we're in a bad mood, we'll see that same situation
completely differently. With awareness, however, we

can notice these emotional filters at play and not be enslaved by them.

In learning how to attune to the emotional life that's here, we can find the choice to apply kindfulness to what's difficult, arousing the strengths of self-compassion and self-love. When we notice positive emotions, we can choose to savor them and allow them to linger until they inevitably pass. Ultimately, we rewire our brains with a sense of confidence that no matter what arises, we can handle it, and it's going to be okay.

Just Do It!

It's amazing what can happen as we start to bring emotional awareness to the forefront of our intention. Just the mere fact of labeling a difficult emotion can make us feel more balanced (Creswell et al. 2007). However, as Rumi said, if we really sit with them, they can be some of our greatest teachers.

Whether you're doing the breathing practice or the body scan, emotions will naturally arise. See what happens as you become curious about them. How are they experienced in the body? What form does the energy take? Does it seem heavy or light? Perhaps it even feels like a certain color. If it feels okay, say to yourself, *It's okay; this emotion is already here; I'll allow myself to feel it.* As you stay with it, does it stay the same or does it change, showing you the impermanence of emotions? Can you picture cradling them and feeling cradled at the same time?

You can also do this in your daily life. As you develop an intimacy with your emotions, you not only build emotional intelligence but also get back into the driver's seat and into that space of choice where learning and possibility lie.

29

♦ ♦ ♦

Let Be and Let Go

In all the classes that we teach, there's a fine line between the experience of "letting be" and "letting go." One of the fundamental attitudes in MBSR is to learn how to "let be." While our default reaction is to try to "do" something about an uncomfortable feeling, the mindful response is to learn how to "be with" what's there. We begin to understand the impermanent nature of our thoughts, emotions, and sensations as we stay with them. Eventually, this can lead to the experience of letting go. However, sometimes we arouse the discernment that it's time to actively let go of something that's there. But this can be even more challenging.

Letting go of an emotion can happen in a few different ways. The unhealthiest way to try to let go of an emotion is through blame. Blame is a mindless reaction the brain uses to try to expel some uncomfortable emotion. We try to shift the discomfort onto someone else or onto ourselves to create the motivation for change. In the end, it backfires.

A healthier way to let go is to try to smile toward the discomfort. Another way is to let it out through crying. If it's anger, go outside and take a rigorous walk. Ultimately, the best way to practice letting go of an emotional stuckness comes back to forgiveness. It helps to have the understanding that everyone on this planet—including us—is a human being and is doing the best he can with what he has.

May we know deeply that we are all fallible human beings. May we learn to let go of the self-blame and unworthiness and begin to forgive ourselves and others.

Just Do It!

Take a moment to consider where you already let go in daily life. Every night you go to sleep, you're letting go; whenever you send a text, you let go; after an embrace, you let go. In the midst of your formal meditation practice, see if you can notice when you're hanging on to something. Maybe you're struggling with staying focused, and in that moment of awareness, you choose to name that experience and let it be. In doing this, you release your grip on it and, at the same time, you are letting go.

Remember that the way we change is through intentional practice and repetition. What would the days, weeks, and months ahead be like if you intentionally practiced and repeated letting be and letting go? As you learn and discern how and when to let go, wisdom begins to grow.

30
♦ ♦ ♦

Turn into the Skid

When I (Bob) was sixteen years old, I got my driver's license. It was a time of new independence and mobility. The world was opening, and I wanted to explore it, but I lived in Boston, and in the winter, I found driving in the snow and ice to be a challenge. When the car started skidding, I would instinctively turn the wheel away from the skid, only to find the car skidding even more out of control.

One day I was discussing this with my dad, and he said, "Bob, if you want to get out of the skid, you need to turn into it." As the New England winter bore on, I started to turn into the skid, and lo and behold, my car would straighten out. I began to realize that I could apply this same principle to other fears and to pain—to whatever I was aversive to. They say that you can run, but you can't hide. I realized that whatever I tried to flee from continued to follow me. As I began to turn into my fears by acknowledging them, I felt a sense of growing freedom. I began to understand that by turning into my fears, I could find my center of balance and deeper freedom.

When living with emotional or physical pain, the tendency is to turn away. "Rid us of this!" we cry. This is, of course, a normal reaction—hardly anyone wants to experience pain. Yet, have you noticed that it often follows you like a shadow?

Although at times turning away or distracting ourselves from pain can be useful, sometimes it just doesn't help. Wouldn't it be good to learn other ways to alleviate pain? What if you could apply the principle of turning into the skid to your emotional or physical pain? This may sound counterintuitive, but what do you have to lose?

Just Do It!

Take a moment to get into a posture in which you feel comfortable and alert, and do a mindful check-in on how you are feeling in your body and mind. If you become aware of any unpleasant feelings, take a moment to acknowledge them.

In turning into the skid of what's present, please use your wise discernment to determine how far you want to skid into your unpleasant feeling. There's no need to go to the high end of the Richter scale of pain; pick something that feels workable and manageable.

As you move into this unpleasant feeling, you may notice the old tendency to turn away, numb out, or go somewhere else. This time, however—if you're up for it—just let it be. Feel and acknowledge what you are experiencing physically, mentally, or emotionally. Notice what happens when you allow and acknowledge what's here. Gradually come back to a few mindful breaths, and then open your eyes, feeling awake and present.

Take a few moments now to write about what came up for you as you began to turn into the skid of fear or emotional or physical pain within your body and mind.

31

♦ ♦ ♦

Mindfulness on the Go

During the day, many of us are moving fast, sometimes physically, but almost always mentally. Our neurons are firing in hyperspeed, with so much to do and so much to pay attention to. We're working so hard to get somewhere that we forget to be here. Sometimes on the way home, if we pay attention, we'll notice that we're "rushing home to relax." In that moment of awareness, we have arrived in the present moment and can choose to "be" different.

A core component to MBSR is mindful yoga and walking meditation. The intention of a mindful movement practice is to show that mindfulness isn't reserved for the cushion. If mindfulness is awareness, you can bring it anywhere, including on the go.

Just Do It!

Here's a four-step moving meditation that can help your brain train in mindfulness while simply walking. Take five, ten, or fifteen minutes out of your day to practice this. Just like with the breathing practice and the body scan, if your mind wanders off, the moment you become aware of that wandering is a congratulatory moment. You are present in a choice point. Simply choose to gently redirect your mind to the practice.

1. *Start with gratitude*—If you are fortunate enough to have the ability to walk, remember that it took you over a year to learn how to walk, and your legs are the unsung heroes that take you to and fro, day in and day out. Thank your legs for all their efforts.

2. *Ground*—Bring your attention to the sensations of your feet and legs as the heel touches the ground, then the sole of the foot, and then the toes, and then the feeling as you lift your weight from that foot. You can say to yourself, *Heel, sole, toes, lift.* This is a way to

connect to the action of walking in the present moment.

3. *Come to your senses*—Walk slightly more slowly and begin to open your awareness to all your senses, one by one: sight, sound, taste, feeling, smell. See what is around you; listen to the sounds; taste the air or what-ever is in your mouth; feel the warmth or coolness of the day, or feel breeze on your cheeks; smell the air. Then stop for a moment and see if you can take in all of the senses.

4. *End with gratitude*—It's essential to end with the acknowledgment that despite what your mind said you would, could, or should be doing, you chose to engage in this practice for your own health and well-being. Take a moment to practice gratitude for yourself and the choice you made.

You can do this practice informally in daily life too, while walking to work, in the hallways at work, running errands, or walking from the car to your front door when you get home. Keep in mind that this is a practice. So whenever you realize that you are rushing home to relax—or really anywhere—just say to yourself, *Rushing, rushing, rushing.* This in itself widens the space between stimulus and response—the space where awareness and choice both lie.

In this space, you are now present and can engage in any of these ways of mindful walking.

But don't just take our word for it; try it for yourself!

32

♦ ♦ ♦

Breath, Body, Sound

One wonderful way we can enter into mindfulness is through the world of sounds. Sounds are vibrations in the atmosphere that the ear picks up and translates into a form that the brain can compute. In our MBSR class, you'll often hear a bell rung to signify the beginning or end of a meditation. As the bell is struck, the metal vibrates—shaking rapidly outward and inward. In the outward movement, it pushes the surrounding air particles, which collide with the particles around them—this is called "compression." In the inward movement, it pulls on the surrounding air particles. This creates a drop in pressure, and like a domino effect, pressure drops on the surrounding particles. This compression and succeeding drop in pressure create a fluctuating wave through the air.

Our ears receive and direct the sound waves, sense the fluctuation in pressure, and turn all this into an electrical signal that one part of the brain can understand as sound—then another part of the brain says, "bell." (This is a very basic and rudimentary description of how we hear; the specifics of it are still quite a mystery to science.)

The process of how we hear and how it all makes sense to our brains is nothing short of one of the great miracles of life. Take a moment right now, pause, and just listen. Whatever you hear, be fascinated by the very fact that you have the ability to hear at all. As we allow our minds to settle into hearing, we start to see that sounds have the same nature as sensations in the body and thoughts. They appear and disappear, and each time one disappears, that sound doesn't leave a trace. There is silence until another sound appears.

Any sound can be the object of our focus. Even the most annoying sounds, like a horn blaring outside, an alarm clock beeping, or people yelling, can be perceived differently when we bring mindfulness to them. The annoyance of those sounds doesn't come from the sounds themselves; it comes from our interpretation of those sounds as "bad." When we bring mindfulness to it, we shift our relationship from aversion to curiosity, allowing the sounds to rise and fall, lessening their negative impact.

Just Do It!

Up to this point, you've experienced mindfulness with the breath and the body scan. It's worth setting some time aside to just sit or lie down and listen to the sounds inside the house, out in the city, or in the contemplative setting of nature. In MBSR we introduce a formal practice that combines the two prior meditations of breath and body that you've experienced with sound in the appropriately titled meditation "breath, body, sound." The beauty of this practice is it builds on the practices you've already been learning. You start with a narrow attention on the breath, then expand out to the body, and then expand further to the world of hearing. You can get an app like Insight Timer to set intermittent bells to tell you when it's time to shift your attention, or just follow the guided audio practice at http://www .newharbinger.com/31731.

1. Begin with awareness of breathing for one to five minutes.

2. Expand from the breath to include sensations in the body for one to five minutes.

3. Widen awareness to include hearing, opening to sounds appearing and disappearing.

As with any of these practices, it's natural for the mind to wander into thinking, and when this happens, simply take note of it and gently guide it back to your intended point of attention.

33

♦ ♦ ♦

Don't Stress About
Your Thoughts

If you've begun to play with the breathing practice or body scan, you've likely noticed how busy your mind is. In part 1, we cued you to pay attention to your thoughts to help feel into the nature of thoughts. But what often comes up when someone begins to practice formal meditation is a struggle between staying focused on the intended point of attention and the incessant busy-ness of the mind. It's as if the mind has a mind of its own, thinking about this, worrying about that, reflecting back onto a memory, or sliding into a dream. This can seem like a frustrating experience in our meditation practice, but that's often because we confuse mindfulness with concentration. Making this distinction is important and will save you a lot of grief. The intention of mindfulness is not to have a laser focus on the breath, body, or sounds; it's to practice being awake. Every time your mind wanders into a story and you notice it, you're practicing mindfulness.

So there's no need to be stressed out by a distracted mind—it's part of the process. In fact, the mind wandering off continues to give us information on what's going on in that mysterious, electrochemical, three-pound bundle of nerve cells we call our brain. Maybe you notice that the mind is rehearsing an upcoming scenario or rehashing a past event. Or you notice certain things make the brain fall into mind traps like catastrophizing, doubting, or blaming. If something is incessantly on the mind, it may mean that it's important to spend more intentional time paying attention to that something.

When we go deeper into the nature of thoughts, sometimes we experience them like a movie. Movies are a series of still frames following each other in rapid succession to create the illusion of moving images. Our eyes retain each frame for a fraction of a second, and the next frame comes so rapidly that we never notice the space between the images. When you pause and pay attention to the mental events of your mind, you'll notice there are a number of images and voices appearing and disappearing constantly, with spaces in between. Some appear to be positive, others negative, and some just neutral.

As we relax the anxiety concerning our thoughts and begin to pay attention to them more closely, we lessen the power of those thoughts and become increasingly better at creating a flexible mind.

Just Do It!

Take a moment to become more intimate with the nature of your thoughts. One way to notice the mental events forming and unforming in your mind is to close your eyes and picture the Golden Gate Bridge or any famous landmark. Picture it in your mind and try to hold it there; see if it stays the same or begins to shift and change a bit. What you'll eventually notice is that our thoughts are akin to a weather system, always shifting and changing, never staying the same. You couldn't hold on to them if you tried.

34

♦ ♦ ♦

Release the Critic

As we continue down the road of any formal mind-fulness meditation practice, it becomes evident that inherent in our human makeup is the mind's need to judge and criticize. Some of us are more naturally talented at this than others. The sad reality is that most of us actually criticize ourselves more than other people. You can hear the voices during your practice: *I'm not doing this right. Others are getting this, but I just can't do it,* or *I'm so bad at meditation.* Our brains do this in some twisted effort to help us figure things out or prepare for some disaster, but rarely—if ever—does it have any beneficial effects. In fact, it usually has the opposite effect, like a slow-leaking toxin in our minds and bodies.

It's worth being curious about how the mental event of criticizing ourselves affects us. Consider for a moment any recent experience in which you had the impulse to criticize yourself. See if you can recall the event—who was there, what was happening, and what happened that ignited the judgment. See if you can get in touch with the emotion behind the judgment. Is there a feeling of shame, sadness, irritation, or maybe tiredness? Usually the urge to criticize ourselves arises out of some uncomfortable emotion we're experiencing in the moment. It's as if the mind's strategy is to use criticizing to get away from what's uncomfortable.

Even bringing mindfulness to the memory can help you become more aware of the cycle of reactivity that comes with judgment. As we see it more often, we can dispel the hold it has on us and open up to a wiser view.

Just Do It!

When you're on the proverbial cushion, be on the lookout for judgment of yourself or others. See if you can name the judgment and sense into the feeling that comes with it. Then gently redirect your attention back to the practice. Notice how often, the judgment and feeling eventually drift away, teaching us about the impermanence of thoughts and emotions.

When you're off the cushion, try spending part of your day noticing whenever judgment comes up in daily life and notice how it affects you physically, mentally, and emotionally. Does it make you happier or not? This practice helps your brain objectify judgment, which naturally makes you feel less identified with it as it arises later on.

Finally, here is the cherry on top. Bringing mindfulness to a comparing mind is a great opportunity to practice a wonderful antidote called "lovingkindness" (see also chapter 42). Lovingkindness is the practice of warming the heart by sending kind intentions to ourselves and others. This practice can have a direct impact on transforming negative mind states like our inner critic.

Whether you're more inclined to judge yourself or other people, see if you can connect to your heart and intentionally wish well for yourself or the other person. This informal lovingkindness practice can be a way to begin nurturing a more benevolent mind and healing the underlying irritation.

Like all things in life, see if you can let any judgments about this practice come and go, and let your direct experience be your teacher.

35

♦ ♦ ♦

Uncover the Comparing Mind

All of us belong to the human race, and really, all beings belong in this universe. There is no such thing as a person who doesn't belong on this planet. The feeling of belonging is a primal need; it brings us a sense of safety and security. We don't have to learn how to belong; we're born with an inherent sense of it. Nevertheless, our brain has a natural tendency to compare ourselves to other people in order to see if we're measuring up or if we belong. This is called the "comparing mind" (a close cousin to the inner critic). This comes up in all areas of life and is highly evident in our meditation practice. What inevitably happens is that, if left unchecked, the comparing mind creates shame, feeding the obstacle of doubt and stopping us in our tracks. It's quite a trick.

Even while reading this book or attempting these practices, you might catch it saying, *I'm not good enough,* or *I'm not a real meditator like John... I'm a fraud.* MBSR groups are fertile ground for this mind state, because there's always a check-in to see how the practice is going. One person may say she's practicing daily, while another has missed doing any formal meditation all week. This is fuel for the comparing mind to insert itself. *Look at Suze. She says she meditates daily; I'll never be able to do that.*

Most of us have to put effort into rediscovering what meditation means to us. For some it's a consistent formal practice of bringing mindfulness to their meals; for others it's the grounding nature of a mindful walk in a park; and still others find refuge in the body scan or lovingkindness practice.

When you notice the comparing mind arising within your practice, heed these words from the late and great poet John O'Donohue:

No one else has access to the world you carry around within yourself; you are its custodian and entrance. No one else can see the world the way you see it. No one else can feel your life the way you feel it. Thus it is impossible to ever compare two people because each stands on such different ground. When you compare yourself to others, you are inviting envy into your consciousness; it can be a dangerous and destructive guest.

Just Do It!

See if you can focus on noting when the comparing mind comes up in your practice and even in your daily life. You'll notice it saying things like, *I suck. I'm not nearly as good a meditator as so and so. I don't have a real meditation practice; I'm not calm and focused.* The first step is simply to identify it in action. As we do this, it becomes a part of our practice, something that arises within our awareness and gives us the opportunity to recognize that this is only a thought that resides within the greater awareness of who we are. The second step is to ask yourself, *What would be here if this thought weren't here?* Might there be more space, more confidence, and more ease with your practice?

Try it out and see for yourself.

36

♦ ♦ ♦

Allow Whatever Is Here

Our meditation practice culminates in the ability to free ourselves from the gripping entanglements of all our stories, sensations, and sounds, and to experience deeper peace and freedom. In MBSR, the final practice that is introduced is called "choiceless awareness." This is an open awareness practice that integrates all previous practices and helps us learn how to stay open and present to the changing conditions of the mind. As we do this, we grow the capacity for acceptance, balance, and the wisdom to see things clearly.

While we can step into choiceless awareness at any moment, the reason we begin with the practices

focused on particular objects of attention is to introduce all the elements of experience and strengthen
the ability to pay attention. Now with this experience we can begin to settle more deeply into a
natural awareness of life as it is. Moment by moment,
we release the need to attend to any one thing and
rest in the timeless present. There is nowhere to go,
nothing to do, no one to be—just here and now,
always.

At one point, the Buddha suggested, "Develop a
mind that is vast like space, where experiences both
pleasant and unpleasant can appear and disappear
without conflict, struggle, or harm. Rest in a mind
like vast sky." It is here where we begin to sense the
boundless freedom that has been there all along.

This doesn't mean that the other meditations
are inferior in any way; it only means that we've
experienced another form of mindfulness meditation. What truly matters is what you learn about
yourself through this practice, as is also the case
with the previous practices. Every one of these
mindfulness practices can lead to a sense of insight

and freedom. The fact is that no one has the corner on the truth of what is best for you—if someone says he does, run in the other direction.

The more you practice, the more you'll learn how to rest in the ungraspable nature of life and open up to a freedom that has been waiting for you all along.

Just Do It!

You can access choiceless awareness anywhere and anytime. Take a few deep breaths and allow this to be a moment to shift from the world of doing into a space of being. Start by opening up to the sounds in the room, and continue with opening awareness to sensations, emotions, and thoughts. Breathe in and open to all that's here; breathe out and allow it all to be as it is. You'll feel how the the trajectory of experience rises and passes away like waves in the ocean. Notice each time the mind grasps on to a sound, thought, or sensation, and say to yourself, *It's like this,* and as it grabs on to something else say, *And this too.* If you ever get lost, come back to the breath and then open your awareness back up from there.

Breathe in, breathe out, you are home.

If you'd like to access a formal choiceless awareness meditation, you can find it at http://www.newharbinger.com/31731.

PART 5

Be

37

♦ ♦ ♦

Living (Loving) Awareness

As we continue to train wholeheartedly in the art of mindfulness, there comes a point at which we begin to realize that there is an uncontrollable, natural rhythm to life. If we try to fight the mental or emotional tornados that come, the more they sweep us away. The more we practice being open to what arises in life, the more life itself becomes a graceful dance. We understand at a deep level the adage "What we resist persists" and that everything that arises "is like this." Even when resistance to the moment comes, "it's also like this." There's no need to grasp on to anything or push anything away;

underneath all the personal reactivity and self-deception lies a deep, open, loving awareness of all that's here. When we stop resisting life, we can hear the whispers beneath the noise and the gifts begin to reveal themselves.

As we let in life as it is and let go of the struggle, a sense of safety and security arises. When painful thoughts or feelings appear within a purely mindful space, compassion naturally follows. When joyful thoughts or feelings are there, they are met with more joy for the joy. When life's challenges tear at the fabric of your being, your practice nurtures a source of refuge and strength. When you realize that behind your eyes is the same awareness that's behind the eyes of your neighbor, your favorite celebrity, the people in war around the world, and even the most hated criminal, the insight and healing experience of connection follows.

At this point, you may have seen glimpses of some of this. Continue to incline your mind to mindfulness and watch as you uncover the loving awareness that has always been there, waiting for you to discover it.

Just Do It!

There are many people who have dedicated their lives to awakening this natural awareness. These are men and women who have cut through the noise and stepped in the middle of the fire of life in order to help alleviate their own suffering and the suffering of the world. One participant in an MBSR class referred to herself as a "mindful warrior"—not in the aggressive sense, but in the sense that she felt great strength and courage to stand in the midst of difficulty with that loving awareness. You can look to other examples like Mother Teresa and Martin Luther King Jr., people who devoted their lives to helping people awaken to the fundamental truth that we are all in this together.

The spiritual teacher Ram Dass has a wonderful practice that gets to the heart of experiencing this loving awareness in daily life. He suggests spending a few moments tapping on the heart and saying, *I am loving awareness, I am loving awareness, I am loving awareness.*

Take a few deep breaths and give that a try right now. Can you feel the essential nature of who you are? What would the days, weeks, and months ahead be like if you could respond to life from this space? Allow the continued courage to meet life with loving awareness to guide you in awakening more and more each day.

38

♦ ♦ ♦

Dip Beneath Identity

A powerful and potentially liberating question to ask yourself is, *Who am I without my story?* We often define ourselves by what we've been told: you're beautiful, smart, ugly, or dumb; you will be successful or you will never amount to anything; you inherited your aunt's anxiety or your mother's smarts. The stories you've learned were shaped in your formative years, and they become your narratives, your definitions of who you think you are. Your story may be inflated with thoughts that you're the greatest, or deflated with thoughts that you're the worst—or perhaps you're just "average."

The task before you is to become mindful of your stories—the narrative you've defined yourself

Be

with and the person who you think you are—and to be open to new possibilities. This may bring you more freedom than you ever imagined from the perspective of this limited definition you've had. At times, these stories—this limited definition of who you are—can be a self-fulfilling prophecy.

Joe was an MBSR student who was brought up to believe he was adequate, that most everything he did was just okay at best and the most he could hope for in life was to be mediocre. He was called "plain looking" and told he had an average intelligence. As time went on, Joe felt hopeless with his lot in life. In class, he was introduced to the body scan and began to look more closely at his life. Joe felt a plethora of emotional and physical pains that were harbored within his body and mind and began acknowledging them. There was tightness, stress, and discomfort in his belly, chest, and jaw.

Being introduced to the sitting meditation and practicing it every day, Joe had an important insight into himself and how he saw the world with a limited definition. When he became mindful of mind states, he realized he was not his thoughts. His thoughts and emotions were constantly changing, but they were not "him." This opened the door to Joe's heart—that he was special and unique and that the limited definition of who he thought he was, was not true. With that realization, Joe saw boundless possibilities and felt deep freedom from the enslavement of his story.

Although we cannot bypass these limited self-definitions, with awareness we can begin to see them more clearly, to not identify with them, and to realize that new potentials abound. Rather than clinging to self-reference, you can open to a self-awareness in which all is possible. It may be scary to ask yourself, *Who am I without my story?*—but it may also be the most liberating question you could ever ask.

Just Do It!

Set your intention to become more mindful of your thought patterns. Are they self-defeating or supportive? Are they life-giving or self-negating?

Try to make it part of your day to do the STOP practice, which is to Stop for a moment, Take a breath, Observe what is happening in your body and mind, and Proceed on with more presence. This is similar to the mindful check-in. You could do either of these practices a hundred times a day to see if you are self-limiting, and if you are, then a hundred times a day bring your mind back to the present moment and see that you were once again lost in your old story. The moment you realize you're not present, you are—and in that moment, you can choose freedom. Make this a daily practice!

39

♦ ♦ ♦

Discover Your Natural Balance

Nancy's story isn't too uncommon. When she stepped into the first class of MBSR, she shared that she had just spent the last six months overseas caring for her sick uncle. She came home for a short respite for a few months. "I've completely lost myself. For quite some time I've been so present to his needs, and now I don't have a sense of myself. I'm angry about that now and hoping this class will help me get that back, but I don't know."

Although caring for others is a compassionate act and gives us a sense of purpose, too much can have the opposite effect. It is called "compassion fatigue." Many studies now show that people who care for elderly, abused, or traumatized patients can become desensitized and less compassionate toward them. It's as if they lose their balance, their equanimity.

In MBSR, we're learning how to practice equanimity, which brings stability, spaciousness, and balance to our hearts and minds. It's the perfect partner to compassion, allowing us to know our pain or the pain of another without getting lost in it or overwhelmed by it. In MBSR, we introduce the mountain meditation to increase this sense of balance and mental stability and to become more intimate with the natural impermanence of life. In this practice, you are guided to imagine yourself as a mountain, staying present to the ever-changing seasons. No matter what weather befalls the mountain, the mountain remains the same. Solid, rooted, and balanced.

After practicing this for a minute, Nancy opened her eyes and said she felt calmer, more relaxed, and more accepting of her vulnerability. She began to understand that beneath the waves of frustration, stress, and vulnerability there was a rootedness she could access. A little while after going back to care for her uncle, she sent an e-mail saying that she was better able to recognize when the severe weather was present and to take care of herself. Sometimes she used the mountain meditation to be present; other times the severity of stress opened her eyes to needing self-compassion for balance. Eventually she gave herself permission to hire a part-time nurse to give her a few hours off here and there.

Just Do It!

Here are a couple variations of the mountain meditation to play with and give yourself the experience of balancing in the midst of life's ever-changing nature.

1. Sit in a comfortable position, close your eyes, and take a few deep breaths. Allow these breaths to be a grounding rod for your body.

2. Imagine yourself as a mountain; imagine the forest covering the mountain, with all its foliage. The more you can embody the sense of being the mountain, the better.

3. Experience the different seasons unfolding—fall, winter, spring, and summer—and how they affect the mountain. Maybe fall has beautiful colors, winter brings snow or ice storms, spring brings new foliage and flowers, and summer brings heat and, potentially, forest fires.

4. Ask yourself, *How has the actual mountain changed?* The mountain remains the same—solid, rooted, and stable.

In the midst of sweeping emotions, be the mountain. "Breathing in, I imagine myself as this mountain; breathing out, I am grounded and solid." Feel into the balance that's there.

40

♦   ♦   ♦

An Optical Delusion
of Consciousness

Albert Einstein is best known as a scientific genius. But in addition to his brilliant intellect, he was a wise man, enthralled by the mysteries of the world and universe. In an excerpt from a letter published in the *New York Post* (1972), he wrote:

A human being is part of the whole, called by us the Universe, a part limited in time and space. He experiences himself, his thoughts and feelings, as something separate from the rest—a kind of optical delusion of his consciousness. This delusion is a kind of prison for us, restricting us to our personal desires and to affection for a few persons nearest to us. Our task must be to free ourselves from this prison by widening our circle of compassion to embrace all living creatures and the whole of nature in its beauty.

Einstein eloquently points to the unity of all things. Matter is made from the basic building blocks of atoms that are found in all material phenomena, so that the idea that anything is separate is, as Einstein puts it, "an optical delusion of consciousness."

Further, he calls this delusion a prison, limiting our lives to self-seeking pleasures and affection to a few people around us. This way of living separates us even more; our world becomes smaller, and our definition of who we are becomes limited (as explored in chapter 38).

As we expand awareness, we begin to get in touch with the world and universe we all share. Quite naturally, our sense of compassion for others and for ourselves begins to expand. We realize that we are a part of a whole and that no one is left out—human and even nonhuman—and we all share the vicissitudes of life, living with the ten thousand joys and ten thousand sorrows.

Just Do It!

Here is an exercise you can do for the next few days or, if you like, for the rest of your life. Make it a practice to help break the spell of delusion that separates you from others. Open your heart to compassion for yourself and to all beings.

1. When getting up in the morning, feel your body...listen to the sounds of birds, fellow humans, or other critters greeting the day. Know that everyone has his or her life and wants to be happy and safe—just like you.

2. When traveling to work, broaden your awareness to all the people on the road and in the trains or buses trying to make a living to support themselves and their families. Include those in the animal world, who are busy gathering food and doing whatever they need to do to live—just like you.

3. At lunchtime, feel the gratefulness that there's food to eat and that all sentient life needs food to live on—just like you.

4. During the day, look around your office or job site or school—or wherever you are—and recognize that we are all in this together. Each of us has feelings; each of us has longings. Take a few moments and open your heart to compassion for all who are around you.

5. Pause for a few moments during the day or night and feel into the world within and around you. How precious it is to be alive and extend your compassion and love to yourself, to the people dearest to you, to all those who you don't know, and to all creatures great and small.

41

♦   ♦   ♦

Consider All Beings

For quite a while now, scientists have acquiesced to the idea that nonhuman animals and even insects hold a certain level of consciousness. Neurobiologists are now finding basic neural nets and the capacity for perception in plants. The sundew plant will catch a fly with incredible accuracy. Some plants close up when ants come to take their nectar, while others, if they are attacked, send out a scent to surrounding plants warning them of danger (Lanza and Berman 2009). Might we have a primitive understanding of what a sentient being really is?

While, of course, nonhuman animals, reptiles, insects, and plants don't have the same capacity for critical thinking that humans do, consider for a moment that they do have the same underlying consciousness. In MBSR, the idea of expanding awareness and positive intentions to all sentient beings comes up when we do the full lovingkindness practice. The practice ends with expanding awareness to all living beings and sending them intentions to be safe, to be healthy, to be happy, and to be at peace. This can seem strange, because why would you ever wish this for a cockroach running through your kitchen? The more scientists drill down into the elements of life, the more they're seeing how truly connected we all are. It follows that the more kindness you show—even to the cockroach—the more kind energy you generate in the world. This lifts not only the cockroach but also you and the rest of us as well.

At this point, you might notice your mental red flags rising up and think we have now gone insane. If you notice those judgments, set them aside for a moment, and let your experience provide the answers. You may not have a cockroach to do this with in your house, but you might do it with a spider or even an ant. Instead of killing it, see what happens when you recognize that this little insect just wants to be safe. Gently capture it and release it in a natural environment.

What do you notice arising within you?

Do you notice an experience of mindfulness, compassion, or maybe even connection? Remember, what we intentionally practice and repeat starts to come automatically, so even if you don't buy into the notion that being kind to a cockroach is somehow the right way of helping the world, use this as an opportunity to nurture these healing capacities within you.

Just Do It!

Try the experiment for a day or a week—act as if all beings matter. If you have a pet, look into his or her eyes, see the awareness behind his or her eyes; it's the same fundamental awareness that is behind yours. When you look at a tree, see if you can sense the consciousness that is there; it moves through time at a very different rate than the rest of us. If you find an insect in your house, you may naturally want to just get rid of it, especially if it's a cockroach.

Instead, consider this insect as a conscious being and gently help it into a safer space.

As you lie down at night, consider for a moment all beings in the universe and say, *May we all feel safe, may we all be healthy, may we all live in peace.*

Prepare for a good night's sleep.

42

♦　　♦　　♦

Lovingkindness

Walt Whitman said, "I am larger and better than I thought. I did not know I held so much goodness." Lovingkindness has been called the antidote to fear. It nourishes loving acceptance and, of all the practices you've learned up to this point, it can have the most immediate impact on changing negative patterns of mind. While the informal heart of lovingkindness is woven throughout MBSR (as it is in this book), in an eight-week MBSR program, the full lovingkindness meditation practice is traditionally introduced in a daylong retreat.

The beauty of this practice is that you can bring it anywhere—at home, to work, or on vacation. As you become more intimate with bringing loving-kindness formally into your life, you inevitably enhance a sense of connectedness not only to your heart but also to life itself.

Just Do It!

Traditionally in the formal practice of lovingkindness, you systematically use a series of friendly intentions toward yourself and others that often come in the form of general phrases such as *May I (or you) be happy, healthy, strong, and free.* While in other MBSR practices the focus of attention was on the breath, body, or sound—or even on holding it all in open awareness—in lovingkindness, the focus is on these kind intentions. The lovingkindness practice outlined below begins with sending these loving intentions to yourself, but if this is challenging, you can also begin with the second or third step—sending these intentions to a teacher or a dear friend or loved one—to kindle the heart, and then come back to you. Inevitably, you will open up these intentions to all beings (see more in chapter 43).

A guided audio download of this practice is available for download at http://www.newharbinger .com/31731.

1. *Start with you*—Start off by sitting or lying down and drawing attention to your heart. Now send these loving intentions inward. *May I be happy; may I be healthy in body and mind; may I feel safe and protected from inner and outer harm; may I be free from fear, the fear that keeps me stuck.*

    It is common that people find it challenging to be kind to themselves. If you find it difficult, pause here, acknowledging the difficulty, and place both hands on your heart as a gesture of caring—a little kindfulness. As you do this, your mind will likely wander onto thoughts, memories, or some outside distraction. That is fine; just note it—it's a moment of mindfulness, a choice point to return.

2. *Follow with people who you consider teachers or benefactors*—Consider a living person who has been a positive source of inspiration

and change in your life. This is someone whom you feel respect for and who elicits feelings of care. This could be a parent, grandparent, or teacher—maybe even someone you've never met but whose lessons have positively impacted you. Now picture that person here, connect to your heart and say to her, *May you be happy; may you be healthy in body and mind; may you feel safe and protected from inner and outer harm; may you be free from fear.* You can also shorten this to *May you be happy, healthy, safe, and free from fear.*

3. *A dear friend or loved one*—Now, picture a person or animal who is alive and whom you care about. Consider what it is that you love about him. Is it his smile, how kind he might be, the way he supports you or is generous in the world? Then, in your mind, picture him in front of you, looking into your eyes, and say to him, *May you be happy; may you be healthy in body and mind; may you feel safe and protected from inner and outer harm; may*

you be free from fear. You can also shorten this to *May you be happy, healthy, safe, and free from fear.*

4. A *neutral person*—This could be the checkout clerk or a neighbor. Though you don't know much about this person, you do know that she wants to be happy, healthy, to be at ease, to be free from fear. Don't worry if the phrases don't fit at this point—just use them as a vehicle to nurture your heart.

5. A *difficult person*—Move on to a difficult person—not someone who caused you any real trauma, but someone who has been irritating or annoying. Picture him and get a sense for his presence. Send him the same wishes you sent the person you care about: *May you be happy, healthy, safe and free from fear.* If this is too difficult, you can always go back to sending lovingkindness or just place your hands on your heart acknowledging the difficulty of the moment and knowing that difficult moments are a part of life, to give a gesture of caring to yourself.

6. *All people and beings everywhere*—Expand this to all people, to all animals, and—if it feels right—to all beings everywhere: *May we all be happy, healthy, at ease and free from fear.*

7. *Conclusion*—As you finish, take a moment to acknowledge yourself for making the effort to engage in this practice for your own health and well-being. This is an act of self-care.

43

♦ ♦ ♦

Opening to Interconnection

According to the big bang theory, we are made of stardust and are connected in very direct and inter-related ways. When you think of interconnection, reflect on this: the very body you are living in is connected to the earth you are living on, which is connected to the solar system and the universe. Not one of those things exists in a void—each is dependent upon the other.

Nothing lives in a vacuum. The world and all of its creatures and plants—great and small—support each other to live. All contribute to the cycles of life. As the earth passes around the sun, the seasons turn, turn, and turn, each supporting the other. A time of growth in spring and summer, and a time for dormancy and revitalization in the fall and winter. Like a vast terrarium, nothing is wasted; all is tied together, feeding and renewing life. Even forest fires fertilize the soil and clear the way for new growth. To not recognize the interconnectedness of things is to live with isolation, fear, loneliness, and separation. May we all grow in wisdom and feel our sense of interconnection with all that is.

Just Do It!

We will end with a closing meditation on interconnection. Settle into a position in which you can either sit or lie down and not be disturbed for ten to fifteen minutes, a position in which you feel awake and comfortable.

Bring awareness to whatever you're sitting or lying upon and feel the sense of contact. Now let your awareness expand to feeling its connection to the floor. Further expand your awareness from the floor to the earth below and feel that connection as well. Taking a few moments, feeling held and connected by this earth.

Now, gently shifting focus and bringing awareness to other senses, become aware of any sounds, smells, sights, and tastes that may be lingering and feel those connections. Feel your aliveness, presence, and being in your senses within your life.

Now, gently shifting the focus, become mindful of breathing in and out. Being present. As you breathe in, appreciate this gift from the plant world that exhales oxygen for you to breathe. Now feel the gift of reciprocation with your exhalation of carbon dioxide, which is a gift to the plants so they can breathe. Feel this interchange of oxygen and carbon dioxide, each supporting another to thrive.

Bring awareness into your own heart, knowing that you are a precious being, that each of us has a place in the world. No one has been forsaken. Feel this sense of connection to your own heart with great tenderness and gradually extend this out to family, friends, community, and to all living beings.

As you come to the end of this meditation and this book, may you know the feeling of being connected in your heart. May you feel your place in this world and your interconnection with all of life. May all beings find the gateways into their hearts and know peace.

References

Baxter, L. R., Jr., J. M. Schwartz, K. S. Bergman, M. P. Szuba, B. H. Guze, J. C. Mazziotta, A. Alazraki, C. E. Selin, H. K. Ferng, P. Munford, and M. E. Phelps. 1992. "Caudate Glucose Metabolic Rate Changes with Both Drug and Behavior Therapy for Obsessive-Compulsive Disorder." *Archives of General Psychiatry* 49(9): 681–89.

Brown, B. 2012. *Daring Greatly: How the Courage to Be Vulnerable Transforms the Way We Live, Love, Parent, and Lead.* New York: Gotham.

Carlson, L. E., M. Speca, P. Faris, and K. D. Patel. 2007. "One Year Pre-Post Intervention Follow-Up of Psychological, Immune, Endocrine and Blood Pressure Outcomes of Mindfulness-Based Stress Reduction (MBSR) in Breast and Prostate Cancer

Patients." *Brain, Behavior, and Immunity* 21(8): 1,038–49.

Carmody, J., and R. A. Baer. 2008. "Relationships Between Mindfulness Practice and Levels of Mindfulness, Medical and Psychological Symptoms and Well-Being in a Mindfulness-Based Stress Reduction Program." *Journal of Behavioral Medicine* 31(1): 23–33.

Christakis, N. A., and J. H. Fowler. 2007. "The Spread of Obesity in a Large Social Network over 32 Years." *New England Journal of Medicine* 357(4): 370–79.

Creswell, J. D., B. M. Way, N. I. Eisenberger, and M. D. Lieberman. 2007. "Neural Correlates of Dispositional Mindfulness During Affect Labeling." *Psychosomatic Medicine* 69(6): 560–65.

Davidson, R. J., J. Kabat-Zinn, J. Schumacher, M. Rosenkranz, D. Muller, S. F. Santorelli, F. Urbanowski, A. Harrington, K. Bonus, and J. F. Sheridan. 2003. "Alterations in Brain and Immune Function Produced by Mindfulness Meditation." *Psychosomatic Medicine* 65(4): 564–70.

Dweck, C. S. 2000. *Self-Theories: Their Role in Motivation, Personality, and Development.* Philadelphia: Psychology Press.

———. 2006. *Mindset: The New Psychology of Success.* New York: Ballantine Books.

Einstein, A. 1972. Letter quoted in the *New York Post.* November 28, 12.

Ekman, P., R. J. Davidson, and W. V. Friesen. 1990. "The Duchenne Smile: Emotional Expression and Brain Physiology II." *Journal of Personality and Social Psychology* 58(2): 342–53.

Emmons, R., and M. McCullough. 2003. "Counting Blessings versus Burdens: An Experimental Investigation of Gratitude and Subjective Well-Being in Daily Life." *Journal of Personality and Social Psychology* 84(2): 377–89.

Farb, N. A., A. K. Anderson, H. Mayberg, J. Bean, D. McKeon, and Z. V. Segal. 2010. "Minding One's Emotions: Mindfulness Training Alters the Neural Expression of Sadness." *Emotion* 10(1): 25–33.

Farb, N. A., Z. V. Segal, H. Mayberg, J. Bean, D. McKeon, Z. Fatima, and A. K. Anderson. 2007. "Attending to the Present: Mindfulness Meditation Reveals Distinct Neural Modes of Self-Reference." *Social Cognitive and Affective Neuroscience* 2(4): 313–22.

Fowler, J. H., and N. A. Christakis. 2010. "Cooperative Behavior Cascades in Human Social Networks." *Proceedings of the National Academy of Sciences of the United States of America* 107(12): 5,334–38.

Fredrickson, B. L., K. M. Grewen, K. A. Coffey, S. B. Algoe, A. M. Firestine, J. M. G. Arevalo, J. Ma, and S. W. Cole. 2013. "A Functional Genomic Perspective on Human Well-Being." *Proceedings of the National Academy of Sciences of the United States of America* 110(33): 13,684–89.

Hölzel, B. K., J. Carmody, M. Vangel, C. Congleton, S. M. Yerramsetti, T. Gard, and S. W. Lazar. 2011. "Mindfulness Practice Leads to Increases in Regional Brain Gray Matter Density." *Psychiatry Research* 191(1): 36–43.

Ito, T. A., J. T. Larsen, N. K. Smith, and J. T. Cacioppo. 1998. "Negative Information Weighs More Heavily on the Brain: The Negativity Bias in Evaluative Categorizations." *Journal of Personality and Social Psychology* 75(4): 887–900.

Kabat-Zinn, J., A. O. Massion, J. R. Hebert, and E. Rosenbaum. 1998. "Meditation." In *Textbook on Psycho-Oncology,* edited by J. C. Holland, 767–79. Oxford: Oxford University Press.

Killingsworth, M. A., and D. T. Gilbert. 2010. "A Wandering Mind Is an Unhappy Mind." *Science* 330(6006): 932.

Kraft, T. L., and S. D. Pressman. 2012. "Grin and Bear It: The Influence of Manipulated Facial Expression on the Stress Response." *Psychological Science* 23(11): 1,372–78.

Lanza, R., and B. Berman. 2009. *Biocentrism: How Life and Consciousness Are the Keys to Understanding the True Nature of the Universe*. Dallas, TX: Benbella Books.

Miller, J., K. Fletcher, J. Kabat-Zinn. 1995. "Three-Year Follow-Up and Clinical Implications of a Mindfulness-Based Stress Reduction Intervention in the Treatment of Anxiety Disorders." *General Hospital Psychiatry* 17(3): 192–200.

Neff, K. 2011. *Self-Compassion: The Proven Power of Being Kind to Yourself.* New York: William Morrow.

Neff, K. D., and C. K. Germer. 2013. "A Pilot Study and Randomized Controlled Trial of the Mindful Self-Compassion Program." *Journal of Clinical Psychology* 69(1): 28–44.

Niemiec, C. P., R. M. Ryan, and E. L. Deci. 2009. "The Path Taken: Consequences of Attaining Intrinsic and Extrinsic Aspirations in Post-College Life." *Journal of Research and Personality* 73(3): 291–306.

Parks, G. A., B. K. Anderson, and G. A. Marlatt. 2001. "Relapse Prevention Therapy." In *International Handbook of Alcohol Dependence and Problems*, edited by N. Heather, T. J. Peters, and T. Stockwell. Sussex, England: John Wiley and Sons.

Poulin, M. J., S. L. Brown, A. J. Dillard, and D. M. Smith. 2013. "Giving to Others and the Association Between Stress and Mortality." *American Journal of Public Health* 109(9): 1,649–55.

Rosenzweig, S., J. M. Greeson, D. K. Reibel, J. S. Green, S. A. Jasser, and D. Beasley. 2010. "Mindfulness-Based Stress Reduction for Chronic Pain Conditions: Variation in Treatment Outcomes and Role of Home Meditation Practice." *Journal of Psychosomatic Research* 68(1): 29–36.

Segal, Z. V., P. Bieling, T. Young, G. MacQueen, R. Cooke, L. Martin, R. Bloch, and R. D. Levitan. 2010. "Antidepressant Monotherapy vs. Sequential Pharmacotherapy and Mindfulness-Based Cognitive Therapy, or Placebo, for Relapse Prophylaxis in

Recurrent Depression." *Archives of General Psychiatry* 67(12): 1,256–64.

Shapiro, S., J. Astin, S. Bishop, and M. Cordova. 2005. "Mindfulness-Based Stress Reduction for Health Care Professionals: Results from a Randomized Trial." *International Journal of Stress Management* 12(2): 164–76.

Shapiro, S. L., G. E. Schwartz, and G. Bonner. 1998. "Effects of Mindfulness-Based Stress Reduction on Medical and Premedical Students." *Journal of Behavioral Medicine* 21(6): 581–99.

Teasdale, J. D., J. M. Williams, J. M. Soulsby, Z. V. Segal, V. A. Ridgeway, and M. A. Lau. 2000. "Prevention of Relapse/Recurrence in Major Depression by Mindfulness-Based Cognitive Therapy." *Journal of Consulting and Clinical Psychology* 68(4): 615–23.

Acknowledgments

From Elisha Goldstein:

So many people are involved in the process of writing a book. I hold deep gratitude for all of my students, patients, teachers, family, and friends—without their connections, this book would not have come into this world. Especially not without the love and support of my wife, Stefanie; my two boys, Lev and Bodhi; and my third little one, who is going to come into this world shortly. Deep, deep bows to Bob Stahl, my coauthor, a wonderful teacher and friend whom I feel so blessed to have been alongside on this journey.

From Bob Stahl:

I want to acknowledge my family, teachers, students, and all creatures great and small with whom I share this wondrous and mysterious universe that we all live in. Deep gratitude to all who have guided me on the path of awareness and heart. Deep bows also to my coauthor, Elisha, a true compadre and good friend.

From Elisha Goldstein and Bob Stahl:

We want to acknowledge Jon Kabat-Zinn for bringing mindfulness-based stress reduction (MBSR) into the world, Stephanie Tade for being a fabulous agent and guide, and all the New Harbinger staff for their care in midwifing this book.

Elisha Goldstein, PhD, cofounded the Center for Mindful Living in Los Angeles, CA. He is coauthor of *A Mindfulness-Based Stress Reduction Workbook*, and author of *Uncovering Happiness: Overcoming Depression with Mindfulness and Self-Compassion, The Now Effect: How a Mindful Moment Can Change the Rest of Your Life*, and *Mindfulness Meditations for the Anxious Traveler*. He developed the Mindfulness at Work™ program recognized by the National Business Group on Health for its success in stress management, the Mindful Compassion Cognitive Therapy (MCCT) program, and the premier eCourse Basics of Mindfulness Meditation, and codeveloped CALM (Connecting Adolescents to Learning Mindfulness) with his wife Stefanie Goldstein, PhD. He is a clinical psychologist in private practice in West Los Angeles, CA.

Bob Stahl, PhD, has founded seven mindfulness-based stress reduction programs at medical centers in the San Francisco Bay Area and is currently offering programs at Dominican Hospital in Los Gatos and El Camino Hospital in Mountain View. Stahl serves as a senior teacher for the Oasis Institute for Mindfulness-Based Professional Education and Training at the Center for Mindfulness in Medicine, Health Care, and Society at the University of Massachusetts Medical School. Stahl is coauthor of *A Mindfulness-Based Stress Reduction Workbook*, *Living with Your Heart Wide Open*, *Calming the Rush of Panic*, and *A Mindfulness-Based Stress Reduction Workbook for Anxiety*. He is the guiding teacher at Insight Santa Cruz and a visiting teacher at Spirit Rock.

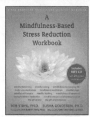

Register your **new harbinger** titles for additional benefits!

When you register your **new harbinger** title—purchased in any format, from any source—you get access to benefits like the following:

- Downloadable accessories like printable worksheets and extra content
- Instructional videos and audio files
- Information about updates, corrections, and new editions

Not every title has accessories, but we're adding new material all the time.

Access free accessories in 3 easy steps:

1. Sign in at NewHarbinger.com (or **register** to create an account).

2. Click on **register a book**. Search for your title and click the **register** button when it appears.

3. Click on the **book cover or title** to go to its details page. Click on **accessories** to view and access files.

That's all there is to it!

If you need help, visit:

NewHarbinger.com/accessories

new harbinger
CELEBRATING
40 YEARS